T0326486

2018 / 2019

EVENTDESIGN JAHRBUCH
EVENT DESIGN YEARBOOK

2018 / 2019

EVENTDESIGN JAHRBUCH
EVENT DESIGN YEARBOOK

Katharina Stein

avedition

INHALT
CONTENT

Events sind aktuell gefragter denn je. In Zeiten von Individualisierung und Selbstinszenierung sind Live-Erlebnisse zum Statussymbol geworden. Fotos vom Burning Man, einer Klettertour oder dem selbst bepflanzten Gemüsegarten posten zu können, macht uns zu etwas Besonderem. Ob Megaevent, eine sportliche Leistung oder das „echte Gefühl", mit den Händen in der Erde zu wühlen.

ERLEBNISSE SIND HOCHEMOTIONALE PROFILIERUNGS-MERKMALE UNSERER GESELLSCHAFT.

Das haben auch andere Marketingbranchen erkannt. So dienen Events heute nicht nur als erlebnisorientierte Basis für verschiedenste Kanäle und Aktionen, sie tauchen auch immer öfter im Portfolio verschiedenster Agenturen auf. Eine Entwicklung all dessen ist die zunehmende Vermischung von Branchen und Kategorien. Events sind als einzelne Marketingmaßnahme immer weniger klar abzugrenzen. Die Formate lassen sich immer seltener eindeutig kategorisieren. Das zeigt sich auch in den Projekten des Eventdesign Jahrbuchs. Klare Grenzen zwischen Branchen, Formaten und Zielgruppen waren in diesem Jahr besonders schwierig zu ziehen.

Kreativdirektor Andreas Horbelt, den ich für diese Ausgabe zum Interview gebeten habe (S. 8), sieht noch eine andere, höchst erfreuliche Begleiterscheinung. Welche genau, soll an dieser Stelle nicht verraten werden, aber so viel sei gesagt: Sie hat mit Zielen und neuen Denkweisen zu tun, die man sich in der Live-Kommunikation schon lange wünscht.

Gleichzeitig wird in diesem Kontext sowie in dieser Ausgabe des Eventdesign Jahrbuchs ein weiterer Aspekt deutlich: Immer mehr Events sind in den – so geliebten oder gehassten – sozialen Medien angekommen. Aber nicht mithilfe banaler Social-Media-Aktionen, sondern mit internettauglichen Inhalten in Gestalt sogenannter Festivals, Summits oder Conferences.

EIN EVENT DIENT NICHT MEHR ALLEINE DAZU, DIE MENSCHEN VOR ORT ZU ERREICHEN, SONDERN CONTENT ZU GENERIEREN, MIT DEM SICH DIE GAST-GEBER UND GÄSTE IN DEN ONLINE-MEDIEN INSZENIEREN KÖNNEN.

Einen zentralen Aspekt nimmt dabei der Raum ein. Er und das gesamte Event müssen „instagramable" sein, wie Andreas Horbelt im Interview näher erklärt. Ein in der Konzeption konsequent anzuwendender inhaltlicher Ansatz, der keiner buchbaren Social-Media-Tools bedarf!

Doch bei aller Freude über diese inhaltsorientierte Entwicklung – Präsenz in den sozialen Medien ist nicht alles. Ein Marketingevent sollte immer noch eine Funktion im Sinne des Gastgebers und Ziele über Posts und Likes hinaus haben. Das Erlebnis und die Menschen vor Ort sollten im Fokus stehen, gerne für Social Media optimiert, aber nicht alleine darauf ausgerichtet. Das, denke ich, wird das nächste, gefährliche und auch schon heute praktizierte Extrem sein, vor dem wir uns tunlichst hüten sollten.

Doch letztlich wird es immer gute und diskutable Events, Entwicklungen oder Extreme geben. Und es wird auch weiterhin so viel Freude bereiten, sich damit kritisch auseinanderzusetzen.

In diesem Sinne, viel Spaß beim Stöbern und Diskutieren der diesjährigen Eventdesigns.

Katharina Stein

EVENTS IM GESELLSCHAFTLICHEN WANDEL
EVENTS AND SOCIAL CHANGE
INTRODUCTION BY KATHARINA STEIN

Events are currently more in demand than ever. In times of individualisation and self-presentation, live experiences have become a status symbol. To be able to post photos of the Burning Man, a climbing tour or a self-planted vegetable garden makes us something special. Whether it is a mega event, a sports performance or the "authentic feeling" of digging in the earth with our hands.

EXPERIENCES ARE HIGHLY EMOTIONAL PROFILING FEATURES OF OUR SOCIETY.

This has also been recognised by other marketing sectors. Events today therefore not only serve as an experience-orientated basis for various channels and actions, but also appear ever more often in the portfolio of various agencies. One by-product of all of this is the increasing blurring of sectors and categories. Events, as individual marketing measures, are less and less clearly delimitable. The formats can now rarely be clearly categorised. This is also evident in the projects in this Event Design Yearbook. It was especially difficult to draw clear boundaries between sectors, formats and target groups this year.

The designer Andreas Horbelt, who I asked for an interview in this edition (p. 8), sees another, highly welcome side effect. Which one exactly will not be revealed here, suffice it to say that it has to do with goals and new ways of thinking that have long been wished for in live communication.

At the same time, another aspect becomes clear in this context and in this edition of the Event Design Yearbook: more and more events have made an appearance in the social media that are so loved or hated. However, not through trite social media actions, but through content suitable for the Internet in the form of so-called festivals, summits or conferences.

AN EVENT NO LONGER SERVES ONLY TO REACH THE PEOPLE AT THE EVENT ITSELF, BUT ALSO TO GENERATE CONTENT WITH WHICH THE HOSTS AND GUESTS CAN PRESENT THEM-SELVES IN ONLINE MEDIA.

The space is a central aspect of this. It and the whole event must be "instagramable", as Andreas Horbelt explains in more detail in the interview. This is an approach to content that must be applied coherently during the conception, which does not require bookable social media tools.

However, as much as one might welcome this content-orientated development – a presence in the social media is not everything. A marketing event should still have a function in the interests of the host and goals beyond posts and likes. The experience and the people attending the event should be the focal point, albeit optimized for social media, but not orientated exclusively towards them. This, I think, will be the next dangerous extreme that is already practiced today and that we should watch out for at all costs.

However, in the end there will always be good and debatable events, developments and extremes. And it will continue to be enjoyable to engage with them critically.

In this spirit, enjoy browsing and discussing this year's event designs.

Katharina Stein

Die Grenzen zwischen u. a. Messe, PR und Event scheinen immer stärker zu verschwimmen. Das fiel uns bei der Durchsicht der diesjährigen Projekte besonders auf. Wie bewerten Sie diese Entwicklung?

Ich erlebe dieses „Verschwimmen der Grenzen" auch in meinem Arbeitsalltag – und ich begrüße es sehr. Ob man eine Messe oder ein Event veranstaltet, ist doch erstmal vollkommen egal und uninteressant. Wichtig ist nur, welche kommunikativen Ziele man erreichen will, warum man also überhaupt eine Maßnahme plant. Wenn man das weiß (und erstaunlich viele Auftraggeber wissen das nicht), dann kann man definieren, wie man diese Ziele am besten mit welchem Format erreicht.

VIELE KUNDEN – LEIDER BEI WEITEM NOCH NICHT ALLE – SIND ENDLICH AN DEM PUNKT ANGE-KOMMEN, DASS SIE NICHT ÜBER FORMATE, SONDERN ÜBER ZIELE NACHDENKEN.

Die strategischen Fundamente für eine Maßnahme und ihre Einbindung in kommunikative Gesamtkonzepte werden immer wichtiger, die Kunden werden selbstbewusster und mutiger, und all das führt eigentlich zwangsläufig zu Hybriden aller Art.

Zwei Beispiele aus dem Umfeld der IAA: Volvo hat sich entschieden, nicht mehr an der Messe teilzunehmen und tourt stattdessen mit einer Art mobilem Messestand durch die Republik. Die Frage, ob das neue Format besser als Minimesse, als Roadshow oder als Event zu beschreiben wäre, ist eigentlich irrelevant. Entscheidend ist: Es gibt überzeugende strategische und kommunikative Gründe dafür, das Format ist erfolgreich und effizient – und hat folglich auch Nachahmer.

Einen ganz anderen Weg hat Mercedes-Benz mit der „me Convention" eingeschlagen, die auch im Buch vorgestellt wird (S. 82): Der Messestand auf der IAA wurde gleichzeitig für ein Festival genutzt, das zusammen mit SXSW® entwickelt wurde. Die Festhalle wurde zum Hybrid aus Messehalle und Eventlocation, der ganz neue Zielgruppen auf das Messegelände lockte – auch das ein kluger, mutiger Schritt, der mit Traditionen und Gewohnheiten gebrochen hat.

Hat das Konsequenzen für die Branche bzw. für jede Agentur?

Gesellschaftliche Umbrüche, veränderte Zielgruppen, Digitalisierung, neue Allianzen und Konkurrenzen, all das zwingt uns, gelernte Formate und Gewohnheiten auf den Prüfstand zu stellen. Nur weil man sich die letzten vierzig Jahre auf einer Messe präsentiert hat oder die letzten zwanzig Jahre mit einem Sales-Meeting begonnen hat, muss man das nicht wieder tun. Der Druck der Veränderung ist auf der Ebene der Formate angekommen – und mutige Kunden wie mutige Agenturen ziehen daraus Konsequenzen.

Für Agenturen bedeutet das: Es trennen sich die Denker von den Machern. Denn wer Formate mitentwickeln will, muss strategisch, konzeptionell und kreativ denken, Altes über Bord werfen und passgenaue Maßnahmen entwickeln. Den Rest erledigen – eine Maßnahme umsetzen – das können viele, die sich noch dazu in einem Marktumfeld bewegen, das unter extremem preislichen Druck steht und nur noch wenig Spaß macht.

Was kommt sonst noch auf die Agenturszene zu?

Der Einfluss von technologischen Lösungen wird weiter zunehmen. Neue Lösungen zu kennen und zu implizieren wird zum Alleinstellungsmerkmal in Wettbewerben. Ich glaube, dass Themen wie BYOD (Bring your own device), Augmented Reality & Virtual Reality, Indoor Navigation, Gesichtserkennung, Robotik, Big Data und Künstliche Intelligenz die Branche noch viel beschäftigen werden. Nicht alles davon ergibt Sinn, manches ist „alter Wein in neuen Schläuchen" oder Innovation um ihrer selbst willen, aber man muss sich diesen Themen (kritisch) stellen. Entsprechend wird die Vernetzung mit Technologiepartnern immer wichtiger. Die Agentur von morgen findet Lösungen nicht mehr alleine, sie ist ein Hub in einem breit aufgestellten partnerschaftlichen Netzwerk von Spezialisten und Experten.

EVENTFORMATE AUF DEM PRÜFSTAND
EVENT FORMATS ARE PUT TO THE TEST
INTERVIEW WITH ANDREAS HORBELT

The boundaries between an exhibition, PR and an event and so on appear to be blurring increasingly. This was particularly evident to us when looking through this year's projects. How do you evaluate this development?

I am also aware of this "blurring of boundaries" in my everyday working life – and I very much welcome it. Whether one is holding an exhibition or an event does not matter at all and is uninteresting in the first instance. What communicative goals one wants to achieve is all that matters, in other words why one is even planning such a measure at all. If one knows that (and a surprising number of clients do not), then one can define how to best reach these objectives and in what format.

MANY CUSTOMERS – UNFORTUNATELY NOT ALL BY ANY MEANS – HAVE FINALLY REACHED THE POINT WHERE THEY ARE NOT THINKING ABOUT FORMATS, BUT ABOUT OBJECTIVES.

The strategic bases for a measure and their incorporation into overall communicative concepts are of increasing importance. Customers are becoming more self-confident and daring, and all of this actually leads inevitably to all kinds of hybrids.

Two examples from the IAA context: Volvo decided not to take part in the exhibition anymore and is touring instead through the republic with a kind of mobile exhibition stand. The question of whether the new format could be better described as a mini exhibition, as a roadshow or as an event is actually irrelevant. What is decisive is: there are convincing strategic and communicative reasons for it, the format is successful and effective – and has emulators accordingly.

Mercedes-Benz, on the other hand, went down quite a different avenue with the "me Convention", which is also presented in the book (p. 82): the exhibition stand at IAA was used at the same time for a festival that was developed together with SXSW®. The festival hall became a hybrid exhibition hall and event location that enticed quite new target groups to the exhibition grounds – also a clever and brave step that broke with tradition and habits.

Does this have consequences for the sector and for each agency?

Social change, changing target groups, digitisation, new alliances and competition – all these force us to question customary formats and habits. Just because one has presented oneself at an exhibition for the last forty years or has started the last twenty years with a sales meeting does not mean one has to do it again. The pressure of change is now also affecting formats – and brave customers and courageous agencies are drawing consequences form that.

For agencies this means that the thinkers distinguish themselves from the doers, because those who wish to contribute to developing formats must think strategically, conceptually and creatively, throw the old overboard and come up with tailor-made measures. Taking care of the rest – implementing a measure – can be handled by many, who furthermore are in a market environment that is under extreme price pressure and is not much fun anymore.

What else is the agency scene facing?

The influence of technological solutions will continue to increase. Knowing and implementing new solutions is becoming a unique selling point in competitions. I believe that topics such as BYOD (Bring your own device), augmented reality and virtual reality, indoor navigation, facial recognition, robotics, big data and artificial intelligence will continue to occupy the sector a lot. Not all of it makes sense, that is for sure, some of it is "old wine in new bottles" or innovation for its own sake, but one has to take a (critical) stance towards these features. Networking with technology partners is of increasing importance accordingly. The agency of tomorrow no longer finds solutions alone, it is a hub in a wide partnership network of specialists and experts.

Auffällig viele Projekte des Eventdesign Jahrbuchs 2018 / 2019 haben bis zu sechs verschiedene Zielgruppen angesprochen. Wie erklären Sie sich diese gehäufte, breite Ausrichtung? Widerspricht sie nicht dem Zeitgeist zu möglichst individuell ausgerichteten Events?

Aus der zunehmenden Individualisierung der Gesellschaft folgt gleichzeitig die Sehnsucht, zumindest für Momente Teil von etwas Großem, Gemeinsamen zu sein. Sonst würden nicht Hunderttausende von Menschen den Kölner Karneval, das Oktoberfest oder den Burning Man feiern.

Marken nutzen diese Sehnsucht für sich, indem sie ihren Stakeholdern Orte und Momente der Identifikation anbieten, indem sie sie für Momente als Gemeinschaft in sich aufgehen lassen – und dafür sind Events perfekt geeignet.

Dass man verschiedene Zielgruppen kombiniert, ist aus Effizienzgesichtspunkten nur naheliegend. Wer den Aufwand betreibt, ein Event auszurichten, will natürlich maximal viele Zielpersonen damit erreichen. Wenn man die Erwartungen der unterschiedlichen Zielgruppen von Anfang an mitdenkt, ist das konzeptionell aus meiner Sicht auch kein Problem. Kundenseitig wird da inzwischen glücklicherweise oft viel ganzheitlicher gedacht und gearbeitet, die alten Gräben zwischen Marketing, PR und Online gibt es so nicht mehr. Maßnahmen werden zusammen gedacht, durchgeführt und Zielgruppen eben auch kombiniert, wenn es Sinn ergibt.

Im öffentlichen Diskurs ist Social Media ein großes Thema. In der Eventpraxis erscheint es eher untergeordnet. Nur selten gehen Events über die übliche „Begleitung durch Social Media oder Influencer" hinaus und schaffen clevere, unkonventionelle Verknüpfungen. Warum?

Ich glaube, Social Media hat einen extremen Einfluss auf die Live-Kommunikation im Hier und Jetzt. Es geht dabei aber nicht um Einladungen an ein paar Influencer oder die Definition lustiger Hashtags – die Veränderungen sind subtiler und fundamentaler.

Zum einen sehe ich eine stetig zunehmende Anzahl von Events, die überhaupt nur noch veranstaltet werden, um Content zu generieren. Die realen Besucher werden – überspitzt gesagt – zur Zielgruppe zweiter Klasse, zu Statisten in Scripted-Reality-Shows, die als Grundlage für einen oder mehrere „dokumentarische" Filme dienen und das Netz viral überschwemmen sollen. Die eigentliche, wesentliche Zielgruppe ist online. Das verändert die Anforderungen an solche Veranstaltungen natürlich extrem: Ob der Weißwein schmeckt, ist eigentlich unerheblich, ob die Besucher einen guten Blick auf die Bühne haben, auch. Hauptsache das Kamerabild stimmt. Den Rest erledigt die Postproduktion.

ZUM ANDEREN VERÄNDERT SOCIAL MEDIA GRUND- SÄTZLICH DIE ART, WIE KONZEPTE ENT- WICKELT UND RÄUME GESTALTET WERDEN – WEIL SOCIAL MEDIA VERÄNDERT, WIE WIR WAHRNEHMEN.

Texte werden kürzer, Botschaften einfacher, Emotionen wichtiger, Räume monumentaler, Dramaturgien schneller: Viele kleine Höhepunkte ersetzen den einen großen Bogen, denn den hält kein Rezipient mehr durch. Botschaften werden in kleinen, gut verdaulichen Häppchen präsentiert. Ein schönes Beispiel dafür ist das Toyota C-HR Festival aus dem aktuellen Eventdesign Jahrbuch (S. 194) . Da war für jeden etwas dabei, das er „liken" konnte ...

A noticeable number of projects in the Event Design Yearbook 2018/2019 appealed to up to six different target groups. How do you explain this multi-layered and wide orientation? Does it not contradict the spirit of the times towards events targeted as individually as possible?

The increasing individualisation of society also brings the yearning to be part of something larger and shared for at least a few moments. Otherwise hundreds of thousands of people would not turn out to celebrate the Cologne Carnival, the Oktoberfest or the Burning Man.

Brands make use this yearning for their own benefit by offering their stakeholders places and moments of identification, by letting them lose themselves for a while as a community – and events are perfectly suited to this.

The fact that one combines various target groups makes sense from an efficiency point of view. Of course, those who make the effort to hold an event want to reach a maximum number of target persons with it. If one considers the expectations of the various target groups from the beginning, it is also no problem conceptually, in my view. Luckily there is currently more holistic thinking and working as regards the customers, so the old delineations between marketing, PR and online no longer exist as such. Combined measures are considered and carried out and target groups are combined accordingly, if it is of benefit.

Social media are a hot topic in public debate. In event practice, however, it appears rather subordinate. It is rare for events to go beyond the standard "accompaniment by social media or influencers" and to create clever, unconventional links. Why?

I think that social media has an extreme influence on live communication in the here and now. It is not about sending invitations to a couple of influencers or defining witty hashtags. The changes are more subtle and fundamental.

On the one hand, I see a steadily increasing number of events that are only held in order to generate content. The real visitors become – to put it bluntly – the second-class target group, background actors in scripted reality shows that serve as a basis for one or more "documentary" films intended to flood the net virally. The actual, significant target group is online. Of course, this significantly alters the demands placed on such events: whether the white wine is good is in fact irrelevant, as well as whether the visitors have a good view of the stage, as long as the camera shot is right. Post production takes care of the rest.

ON THE OTHER HAND, SOCIAL MEDIA IS BASICALLY CHANGING THE WAY THAT CONCEPTS ARE DEVELOPED AND SPACES ARE DESIGNED – BECAUSE SOCIAL MEDIA CHANGES WHAT WE PERCEIVE.

Texts are getting shorter, messages simpler, emotions more important, spaces more monumental, dramaturgies faster: many little highlights replace the one protracted feature, as no recipient will sit through it anymore. Messages are presented in small, easily digestible bites. A good example of this is the Toyota C-HR festival in the current Event Design Yearbook (p. 194). There was something for everyone to "like" ...

Viele aktuelle Events und auch viele Projekte aus dem Eventdesign Jahrbuch bestechen vor allem durch die räumliche Gestaltung. Warum scheint der Fokus vieler Events auf dem Raum zu liegen?

Grundsätzlich glaube ich: Gestaltung wird immer wichtiger. Und auch das ist eine Folge unserer veränderten Wahrnehmung. Es geht um große, überraschende Bilder, in die ich als Besucher immersiv eintauchen kann. Details werden unwichtiger, es zählt die große, einfache Geste. Überspitzt gesagt: Twitter hat die Sprache auf 140 Zeichen reduziert, Instagram reduziert Räume auf Selfie-Hintergründe. Und damit wir uns nicht falsch verstehen: Das macht die Sache nicht einfacher.

DIE MENSCHEN WOLLEN SICH IN UNGEWÖHNLICHEN, ÜBERRASCHENDEN SZENARIEN ERLEBEN UND FOTOGRAFIEREN. DESWEGEN MÜSSEN RÄUME ZUALLERERST UND VOR ALLEM „INSTAGRAMABLE" SEIN.

Momentan sieht man besonders viele industrielle Eventdesigns: Industriehallen, Möbel aus Europaletten, unbehandelte Spanplatten, Schiffscontainer u.s.w. Welche Elemente wird man auf künftigen Events häufig sehen?

Für die Gestaltung der nächsten Jahre sehe ich ein paar mögliche Trends: Szenografien werden spielerischer. Räume werden Spielplätze. Sie laden uns ein, in überraschenden Situationen und Umgebungen aufzugehen, ob medial oder analog. Rutschen zum Beispiel, klassische Accessoires des Kinderspielplatzes, werden zu wiederkehrenden Elementen von Veranstaltungen und Ausstellungen.

Dasselbe gilt für den Spiegel. Wie kein anderes Gestaltungselement lädt er dazu ein, überraschende Räume zu gestalten, die mit Perspektiven und Einblicken spielen. Gleichzeitig kann man den Spiegel als simples Serviceangebot lesen: Komm her und fotografiere dich!

Ein anderer Weg, mit einfachen Mitteln große Bilder zu erzeugen, sind Farben. Colorblocking, große monochrome Flächen oder „laute" Farbkombinationen sind eine einfache Möglichkeit, überraschende fotogene Räume zu schaffen. Ein beeindruckender Vorreiter dieser Entwicklung hin zu starken Bildern ist der Olympus Perspective Playground, den man auch aus dem Eventdesign Jahrbuch kennt (S. 92). Aus meiner Sicht eines der besten und überraschendsten Eventkonzepte der letzten Jahre.

Und dann steht sicher auch das nächste Jahr noch unter dem Oberthema „Wärme und Menschlichkeit". Marken wollen – anders als so mancher CEO – keine unnahbaren Götter mehr sein, sondern ein Teil unserer Lebenswelten und unseres Lebens. Das bewährte Mittel der Wahl: Holz, Holz, Holz und Pflanzen, Pflanzen, Pflanzen. Wetten?

Andreas Horbelt, vielen Dank für das interessante Interview! (Das Interview führte Katharina Stein.)

Andreas Horbelt arbeitet als freiberuflicher Kreativdirektor für Events, Messen, Showrooms, Markenausstellungen und Expo Pavillons. Der studierte Theaterwissenschaftler war von 2005 bis 2010 Kreativdirektor bei Triad Berlin und danach bis 2015 Chief Creative Officer bei Uniplan. Als Mitglied des ADC und DDC verfügt er über langjährige internationale Erfahrung und ist vielfach ausgezeichnet worden. 2017 entwickelte er als Kreativdirektor für insglück den Deutschen Pavillon für die EXPO in Kasachstan.

www.v-effekt.de

Many current events, as well as many projects from the Event Design Yearbook distinguish themselves especially by their spatial design. Why does the focus of many events appear to be on the space?

Basically, I believe that design is of increasing importance. And that, too, is a consequence of our changed perception. It is about large, surprising images that visitors can immerse themselves in. Details are becoming less important, what matters is the sweeping, simple gesture. Case in point: Twitter has reduced language to 140 characters, Instagram reduces spaces to selfie backgrounds. And to make sure there is no misunderstanding: this does not make the matter simpler in any way.

PEOPLE WANT TO EXPERIENCE AND PHOTOGRAPH THEMSELVES IN UNUSUAL, SURPRISING SCENARIOS. THIS IS WHY SPACES MUST COME FIRST AND ESPECIALLY BE "INSTAGRAMABLE".

Currently one can see a lot of industrial event designs, in particular: industrial halls, furniture made of europallets, untreated chipboard, ship containers etc. What elements will be seen frequently at future events?

For the design of the forthcoming years, I can a couple of possible trends: scenography will become more playful. Spaces become playgrounds. They invite us to lose ourselves in surprising situations and surroundings, whether medial or analogue. Slides, for example, the traditional accessories of children's playgrounds, are becoming recurring elements of events and exhibitions. The same applies to the mirror. Like no other design element, it invites one to design surprising spaces that play with perspectives and insights. At the same time, one can interpret the mirror as a simple service offer: come here and photograph yourself!

Another way to create great images with simple means is colour. Colour blocking, large monochrome surfaces or "loud" colour combinations are a simple possibility for creating surprising, photogenic spaces. An impressive forerunner of this development towards powerful images is the Olympus Perspective Playground, which we also know from the Event Design Yearbook (p. 92) . In my view, one of the best and most surprising event concepts in recent years.

And then next year will no doubt also still be under the leading theme of "warmth and humanity". Brands – contrary to some CEOs – do not want to be unapproachable gods anymore, but part of our worlds and life. The proven means of choice: wood, wood, wood and plants, plants, plants. Want to bet?

Andreas, many thanks for the interesting interview! (The interview was conducted by Katharina Stein.)

Andreas Horbelt works as a freelance creative director for events, exhibitions, showrooms, brand exhibitions and Expo pavilions. After theatre studies, he was Creative Director at Triad Berlin from 2005 to 2010 and then until 2015 Chief Executive Office at Uniplan. As a member of ADC and DDC, he has many years of international experience and has won many awards. In 2017, as Creative Director for insglück, he developed the German pavilion for EXPO in Kazakhstan.

www.v-effekt.de

Jede Zielgruppe hat unterschiedliche Bedürfnisse und Erwartungen. Dementsprechend sind Eventkonzepte im Idealfall nicht nur auf den Absender, sondern vor allem auf die Empfänger zugeschnitten.

PUBLIC: EINE BREITE ÖFFENTLICHKEIT, DIE SICH AUS EINWOHNERN, TOURISTEN, PASSANTEN, FLANEUREN ETC. ZUFÄLLIG ZUSAMMENSETZT. DEMENTSPRECHEND HETEROGEN – IN (SOZIALER) HERKUNFT, ALTER ODER VORLIEBEN – ZEIGT SICH DIESE ZIELGRUPPE, DIE NICHT NUR SEHR GROSS, SONDERN IN DER ANSPRACHE NICHT EINDEUTIG ZU FASSEN IST. WAS DEN JEWEILIGEN PERSONEN ALLERDINGS GEMEIN IST, IST EIN NICHT KOMMERZIELLES INTERESSE.

Each target group has different requirements and expectations. Event concepts are therefore ideally not only geared towards the addressor, but especially towards the recipients.

PUBLIC: A WIDER PUBLIC IS COMPOSED BY CHANCE OF INHABITANTS, TOURISTS, PASSERS-BY ETC. THIS TARGET GROUP IS HETEROGENEOUS ACCORDINGLY – IN TERMS OF (SOCIAL) BACKGROUND, AGE OR PREFERENCES – AND IS NOT ONLY VERY LARGE, BUT ALSO DIFFICULT TO GRASP IN TERMS OF APPEAL. HOWEVER, WHAT THESE PEOPLE HAVE IN COMMON IS A NON-COMMERCIAL INTEREST.

FRAUNHOFER JAHRESTAGUNG – EXTENDED
ONLIVELINE GMBH, COLOGNE

Location
Dresden City, Dresden

Client
Fraunhofer-Gesellschaft zur Förderung der angewandten Forschung e.V., Munich

Month / Year
May 2017

Duration
several days

Dramaturgy / Direction / Coordination
onliveline GmbH - Büro für Konzept & Inszenierung, Cologne

Media
media 3, Essen (Award ceremony); congaz, Dusseldorf (façade projection); onliveline Gmbh - Büro für Konzept & Inszenierung, (Animation); Felix Wolff (Laser), Berlin

Music
Matz Flores, Dusseldorf

Lighting
Nik Evers, Wuppertal

Artists / Show acts
Denis Geyersbach, Leipzig; Nadine Geyersbach, Bremen; Jonathan Schimmer, Cologne; Julia Dillmann, Dusseldorf; Miguel Abrantes Ostrowski, Munich; Takao Baba, Dusseldorf; Rachel Ensor, London

Decoration
satis&fy AG, Karben

Others
pms professional media service, Dresden (Technology); satis&fy AG (Technology); Kati Kolb, Wiesbaden (Costumes); Hanns Noelle, Schwelm (Programming)

Photos
onliveline GmbH - Büro für Konzept & Inszenierung, Cologne

Traditionell lag der Fokus der Fraunhofer Jahrestagungen bisher auf einer exklusiven Abendveranstaltung und Preisverleihung. 2017 galt es jedoch, die Marke Fraunhofer zu stärken und den unterschiedlichsten Zielgruppen näherzubringen – real und digital. In diesem Sinne erweiterte onliveline den Fokus, teilte die Jahrestagung in drei Veranstaltungen auf und verknüpfte sie mit einer übergeordneten, als Verbindungsstück dienenden Online-Plattform. Diese Website bot einen erstmaligen, themenorientierten Zugang zu allen 69 Instituten – eine onlinebasierte, ganzheitliche Markenpräsentation, die alle Forschungsfelder sowie einzelne Projekte vorstellte. Intern fungierte sie darüber hinaus als institutsvernetzende Plattform und Kundenakquise-Tool.

AUS EINEM EVENT WERDEN DREI – MIT EINEM VERBINDENDEN DIGITALEN KONTAKTPUNKT FÜR UNTERSCHIEDLICHSTE ZIELGRUPPEN.

The focus of the Fraunhofer annual conventions was traditionally an exclusive evening event and prize award ceremony. In 2017, however, it was about strengthening the Fraunhofer brand and reinforcing it among a wide range of target groups – both real and digital. In the interests of this, onliveline widened the focus, divided the annual convention into three events and linked them by means of an overarching online platform, serving as a connecting element. This website offered initial theme-oriented access to all 69 institutes – an online-based, overall brand presentation that presented all research fields and individual projects. Internally it also functioned as a networking platform for the institute and as a customer acquisition tool.

In Dresden, wo 13 Fraunhofer Forschungseinrichtungen ansässig sind, begann die Kampagne mit einer öffentlichen und ungewöhnlichen Stadtführung. Inhaltlich führte sie die Geschichte der Stadt Dresden mit den Geschichten der Fraunhofer-Institute zusammen. An sechs Schauplätzen wurden bedeutende Erfindungen mit den Forschungsergebnissen der Fraunhofer-Institute in Szene gesetzt – teils von Schauspielern erzählt, mithilfe von Fassadenprojektionen inszeniert oder durch Gespräche und Austausch erklärt. In einer Wanderausstellung, in der die digitalen Inhalte der Online-Plattform haptisch zugänglich wurden, konnten Kunden und Mitarbeiter das Institut und seine Arbeit kennenlernen. Projekte, Objekte, Vernetzung und Historie der einzelnen Forschungseinrichtungen wurden begehbar nähergebracht. Eine exklusive Abendveranstaltung und Preisverleihung griff einzelne Projekte heraus und inszenierte sie real-digital.

ONE EVENT BECOMES THREE – WITH A LINKING DIGITAL CONTACT POINT FOR A WIDE VARIETY OF TARGET GROUPS.

In Dresden, the seat of 13 Fraunhofer research facilities, the campaign started with a public and unusual guided tour of the city. Its content brought together the history of the city of Dresden and the stories of the Fraunhofer Institutes. Significant inventions resulting from Fraunhofer Institutes' research were staged in six locations – sometimes narrated by actors, presented with the help of façade projections, or explained through discussions and exchanges. Customers and personnel could get to know the institutes and their work haptically at a touring exhibition. Projects, objects, networking and the history of the individual research facilities were presented as a walk-in event. An exclusive evening event and prize award ceremony highlighted individual projects and presented them through both real and digital media.

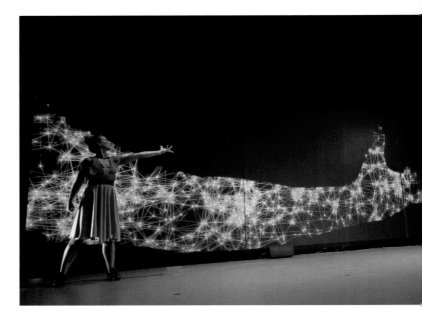

LE BALLET DES OMBRES HEUREUSES
ACTLD, BRUSSELS

Location
Place du Château, Strasbourg

Client
Ville de Strasbourg, Strasbourg

Month / Year
July – September 2017

Duration
10 weeks

Dramaturgy / Direction / Coordination / Architecture / Design / Lighting
ACTLD, Brussels

Graphics
ACTLD; LIMELIGHT, Budapest

Music
Musicom, Brussels

Decoration
FX³, Beauchvechain

Realisation
PRG Belgium, Brussels (Lighting); ADC Productions SA/NV, Zaventem (Video); Lagoona Strasbourg, Schiltigheim (Sound)

Others
Rosco, London (Glass gobos)

Photos
Didier Boy de la Tour, Paris

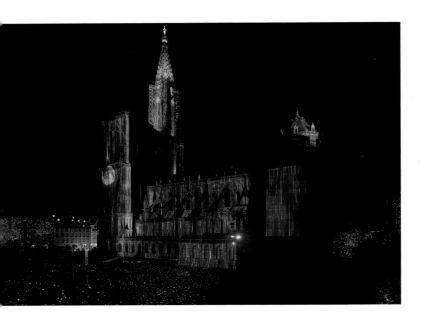

MIT ZEITGENÖSSI-SCHER TECHNIK WIRD DIE ALTE TRADITION DES SCHATTENSPIELS WIEDERBELEBT UND EIN IMMERSIVES ERLEBNIS ERZEUGT.

Von Juli bis September 2017 wurde das Liebfrauenmünster zu Straßburg (Cathédrale Notre-Dame de Strasbourg) erneut zur Kulisse einer überdimensionalen Illumination. Die Klang- und Lichtshow mit dem Namen „Le Ballet des Ombres Heureuses" (Das Ballett der glücklichen Schatten) wurde in diesem Jahr von der alten Tradition des Schatten-spiels inspiriert. Ein Schauspiel aus Licht und Schatten, wie es die Kathedrale selbst seit Jahrtausenden bietet, war zentrales Ausdrucksmittel, um ein immersives 360-Grad-Erlebnis zu erschaffen. Die Silhouette der Kathedrale übernahm die Rolle des Geschichtenerzählers. Ihre Formen und Umrisse schienen sich durch das Schattenspiel immer wieder zu wandeln und erzählten auf diese Weise kontrastreiche, poetische Geschichten.

From July to September 2017, the Cathédrale Notre-Dame de Strasbourg was once again the backdrop for a large-scale illumination. The sound and light show called "Le Ballet des Ombres Heureuses" (The Ballet of Happy Shadows) was inspired this year by the old tradition of shadow theatre. A spectacle of light and shadows, like the cathedral itself has been offering for millennia, was the central expressive medium for creating an immersive 360° experience. The silhouette of the cathedral took on the role of the storyteller. Its shapes and contours appeared to transform continuously during the shadow play, as a way of telling contrasted, poetic tales.

WITH CONTEMPO-RARY TECHNOLOGY, THE OLD TRADITION OF SHADOW THEATRES WAS RE-VIVED, GENERATING AN IMMERSIVE EXPERIENCE.

Die Lichtdramaturgie entwickelte sich allmählich von Schwarz und Weiß zu farbigen Szenen. Die weißen Töne verstärkten die ursprüngliche Farbe der Steine, während die Farben sanft zum Vorschein kamen und die Zuschauer durch faszinierende Universen führten. ACTLD entwickelte in enger Zusammenarbeit mit Rosco das Spiel aus Licht und Schatten mithilfe von 330 Glas-Gobos (graphical optical blackout). Das Schattenspiel erweiterte das farbenprächtige Mapping sowie die darauf abgestimmten rhythmischen Klangwelten. Im Sinne eines authentischen Erlebnisses lag ein besonderes Augenmerk darauf, dass alle technischen Elemente im Hintergrund standen und den Zuschauern verborgen blieben. Hierfür wurden eigens gebaute Set-Elemente installiert.

The dramaturgy of light evolved gradually from black and white to coloured scenes. The white tones enhanced the original colour of the stones, while the colours emerged softly and led the spectators through fascinating universes. In close cooperation with Rosco, ACTLD developed the play of light and shadow using 330 glass gobos (graphical optical blackouts). The shadow play extended the richly colourful mapping, as well as the rhythmic sound worlds coordinated with them. In the interests of an authentic experience, particular attention was paid to ensure that all the technical elements were in the background and concealed from the spectators. Specially made additional set elements were installed for this purpose.

#PUREVELAR TOUR
VOSS+FISCHER GMBH, FRANKFURT A. MAIN

Location
MS OTRATE, several german cities

Client
Jaguar Land Rover Deutschland GmbH, Kronberg

Month / Year
May – July 2017

Duration
several weeks

Dramaturgy / Direction / Coordination / Architecture / Design
VOSS+FISCHER GmbH, Frankfurt a. Main

Graphics
VOSS+FISCHER GmbH; Spark44 GmbH, Frankfurt a. Main

Lighting
Neumann&Müller Gmbh & Co. KG, Frankfurt a. Main

Media / Films
Jaguar Land Rover Deutschland GmbH

Decoration
MDL Expo International GmbH, Trebur

Catering
Gaumenfreund by H-Hotels.com, Berlin

Realisation
VOSS+FISCHER GmbH

Others
APS GmbH, Wülfrath; Rhenus PartnerShip GmbH & Co. KG, Berlin; Rosemeier Schiffbau GmbH, Minden

Photos
Jaguar Land Rover Deutschland GmbH, Kronberg

PURISMUS UND SKULPTURALES DESIGN SETZEN EINEN BEWUSSTEN FOKUS AUF DEN VELAR UND EINEN UNGESTÖRTEN ERSTKONTAKT.

Man muss nicht immer schreien, um gehört zu werden. Diesen Grundsatz kann man auch im Eventdesign adaptieren. Ein Beispiel dafür liefert die deutschlandweite Einführungstour des Range Rover Velar. Basierend auf dem Kick-off-Event in einem reflexionsarmen Raum (allgemeinsprachlich: schalltoten Raum) der TU München, entwickelte VOSS+FISCHER ein Konzept mit dem bewussten Fokus auf Purismus und skulpturalem Design. Das ebenso schlichte Frachtschiff „MS Otrate" diente als Location auf dem Wasser, sollte die Neugierde der Zielgruppe wecken und im Verlauf der Tour verschiedene Ziele anfahren.

One does not always have to shout to be heard. This principle can also be applied to event design. The Germany-wide introductory tour for the Range Rover Velar provides an example of this. Based on the kick-off event in an anechoic room at TU Munich, VOSS+FISCHER developed a concept with a conscious focus on purism and sculptural design. The equally sleek freight ship MS Otrate also served as a venue on the water and was designed to awaken the curiosity of the target group, heading to various destinations over the course of the tour.

PURISM AND SCULPTURAL DESIGN PLACE A CONSCIOUS FOCUS ON THE VELAR AND ENSURE AN UNDISTURBED INITIAL CONTACT.

Die Präsentation im Bauch des Schiffes führte durch zwei aufeinander aufbauende Bereiche. Im ersten Raum wurden die technischen Besonderheiten des Wagens vorgestellt. Ein dezent gestalteter Wandelgang aus halbtransparenten Dreiecken diente als räumliche Einleitung und erster Kontaktpunkt zu den Facetten des Velar. Am Ende öffnete sich ein komplett in Weiß gehaltener Bereich, der sensorischen Freiraum für die puristische Präsentation des Autos lassen sollte. Bei der akustischen Erkundung konnten Besucher den Wagen losgelöst von allen Umgebungsgeräuschen erleben. Noice-Cancellation-Kopfhörer sorgten für die Zuspielung von Audioinhalten und gleichzeitige Ausfilterung aller Umgebungsgeräusche. Der sich aus dem reflexionsarmen Raum ergebende und zurückhaltende Ansatz fand sich im gesamten Design wieder. Schriftzüge, Logos und Grafiken wurden auf den vier Meter hohen Wänden in Weiß auf Weiß foliert. Glänzende Motive auf mattem Untergrund schufen den einzigen und nur bei bestimmten Lichteinflüssen leicht erkennbaren Kontrast.

The presentation in the hold of the ship led through two areas, one of which built on the other. In the first area, the special technical features of the car were presented. An ambulatory with a modest design made of semi-transparent triangles served as a spatial introduction and as a first contact point with the facets of the Velar. An area completely in white opened up at the end, intended to leave sensory space for the purist presentation of the car. Visitors were able to experience the car isolated from all ambient noise, as an acoustic exploration. Noise cancellation headphones played audio content and at the same time filtered out all ambient noise. The reserved approach of the anechoic space was reflected in the whole design. Lettering, logos and graphics were stretched on foil over the four-metre-high walls in white on white. Shiny motifs on a matt background created the only slight contrast, only recognisable in certain lighting conditions.

MAYA – A MIXED REALITY TECHNO OPERA
MATHIS NITSCHKE, MUNICH

Location
Ruins of the Aubing thermal power plant, Munich

Client
Mathis Nitschke, Munich

Month / Year
October 2017

Duration
several days

Dramaturgy
Thomas Jonigk, Berlin

Direction / Coordination / Music
Mathis Nitschke

Graphics
Anja Gerscher, Munich

Lighting
Urs Schönebaum, Munich

Media
Klasien van de Zandschulp, Amsterdam; Luciano Pinna, Amsterdam

Films
Felix Hentschel, Munich

Artists / Show acts
Martina Koppelstetter, Munich; TrioCoriolis, Gräfelfing

Catering
Trisoux Bar, Munich

Others
Katharina Dobner, Regensburg (Costumes); Martina La Ragione, Bologna (Choreography)

Photos
JULIA HILDEBRAND & INGOLF HATZ PHOTOGRAPHERS, Munich; Mathis Nitschke, Munich

Heutige Möglichkeiten bieten der Live-Kommunikation große Freiheiten, zu experimentieren – seien es neue Technologien, die Auswahl an außergewöhnlichen Orten oder die Offenheit und Neugierde der Menschen. Leider werden diese Chancen nur selten so kreativ und frei von Konventionen ausgeschöpft, wie es bei MAYA der Fall war. Die Augmented-Reality-Oper von Mathis Nitschke bot ihren Besuchern im ehemaligen Heizkraftwerk Aubing einen unkonventionellen und detailverliebten Kosmos an Eindrücken. Live-Musik, Sound, Licht, digitale Kunst und eine Geschichte, die aus dem spezifischen Ort heraus entwickelt wurde, ohne hinzugefügte Requisiten oder Bühnen. Der Besucher ging dabei auf aktive Entdeckungsreise und bekam die Freiheit, die begehbare Post-Utopie mithilfe einer Augmented-Reality-App selbst zu erkunden.

Present-day possibilities offer live communication a wide scope of freedom to experiment – whether it is new technologies, the choice of exceptional locations, or the openness and curiosity of the people. Unfortunately, these opportunities are rarely exploited as creatively and as free of convention as was the case for MAYA. The Augmented Reality opera by Mathis Nitschke offered its visitors in the former thermal power station Aubing an unconventional and detailed cosmos of impressions, with live music, sound, light, digital art and a story that was developed from the specific location, without the addition of props or stages. Visitors went on an active journey of discovery and were given the freedom to explore the walk-in post-utopia themselves with the help of an Augmented Reality app.

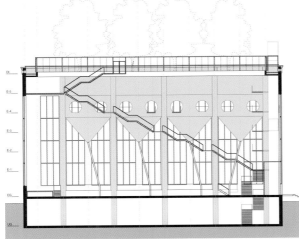

DIGITALE KUNST, AUGMENTED REALITY UND EIN MULTI-SENSORISCHES ABEN-TEUER MACHTEN AUS KONSUMENTEN AKTIVE ENTDECKER.

DIGITAL ART, AUGMENTED REALITY AND A MULTISENSORY ADVENTURE TURN CONSUMERS INTO ACTIVE EXPLORERS.

MAYA erzählte die Geschichte der letzten Überlebenden einer dem Untergang geweihten Zivilisation. Rätselhafte Spuren deuteten auf eine vergangene und gescheiterte Zukunft hin, in der Mensch und Maschine zu einer Einheit verschmolzen waren – zu menschlichen Avataren, über deren Herkunft und Geschichte nur die gleichnamige Figur Maya, die letzte ihrer Art, hätte Auskunft geben können. Jeder Hinweis bespielte den Raum neu, Maya tauchte immer wieder woanders auf und das Publikum folgte ihr in immer neuen Konfigurationen. Das einzigartige Musiktheaterstück griff aktuelle Fragen unserer Zukunft auf und verarbeitete sie als multisensorisches Science-Fiction-Abenteuer auf mehreren Realitätsebenen. Vergangenheit, Gegenwart und Zukunft begegneten einander. Stofflichkeit traf auf Imma-terialität. Reale und digitale Erlebnisräume verschmolzen zu einem in der Form und an dem Ort einmaligen Erlebnis.

MAYA told the story of the last survivors of a doomed civili-sation. Mysterious traces indicated a past and failed future, in which man and machine had merged into an entity. There were human avatars, about whose origins and history only Maya, the figure of the same name and the last of her kind, could have provided information. Every clue played on the space anew, Maya kept reappearing somewhere else and the public followed her in constantly changing configurations. The unique musical theater piece took up current questions about our future and presented them as a multisensory science-fiction adventure on multiple reality levels. It was a meeting of the past, present and future. Materiality met immateriality. Real and digital experiences merged to an experience that was unique in terms of its form and location.

HEIMATGENERATOR –
VITRA AMPELPHASE 8
ATELIER MARKGRAPH GMBH, FRANKFURT A. MAIN

Location
Vitra GmbH – Showroom Frankfurt,
Frankfurt a. Main

Client
Vitra GmbH – Showroom Frankfurt

Month / Year
August – September 2017

Duration
several weeks

Architecture / Design
Atelier Markgraph GmbH, Frankfurt
a. Main

Media
Bildwerk Media, Vienna (Programming /
Web application)

Photos
Holger Peters / Vitra GmbH – Showroom
Frankfurt, Frankfurt a. Main; Kristof Lemp,
Darmstadt

EINE INTERAKTIVE UND SPIELERISCHE ANREGUNG, DEN WIDERSPRÜCHLICHEN BEGRIFF „HEIMAT" ZU REFLEKTIEREN.

Seit 2007 stellt Vitra ausgewählten Architektur- und Gestaltungsbüros die großflächigen Schaufenster des Frankfurter Showrooms für kreative Projekte zur Verfügung. Jeweils drei Wochen lang werden Passanten und Autofahrern verschiedenste Installationen geboten, um sich die Wartezeit an der Ampel zu vertreiben. Als Beitrag zur 2017 stattfindenden Ampelphase 8, die „Heimat" zum Thema hatte, entwickelte Atelier Markgraph eine interaktive Schaufensterinstallation.

Since 2007, Vitra have been making the large display windows of the Frankfurt showroom available to selected architecture and design offices for creative projects. For three weeks at a time, passers-by and car drivers are offered widely varying installations, to pass the time while waiting at the traffic lights. Atelier Markgraph developed an interactive display window installation as a contribution to traffic light phase 8 that took place in 2017, on the topic of "homeland".

AN INTERACTIVE AND PLAYFUL STIMULUS TO REFLECT ON THE CONTROVERSIAL NOTION OF "HOMELAND".

„Heimat" ist ein heute viel diskutiertes, aber bei genauerer Betrachtung schwer greifbares Wort. Um eine spielerische Diskussion über die Bedeutung und Vielschichtigkeit unserer Heimat-Vorstellungen anzuregen, entwickelte Atelier Markgraph den sogenannten HEIMATGENERATOR – ein Automat, dessen visuelle Gestalt bereits mit deutschen Klischees spielt. Der an eine Kuckucksuhr angelehnte Generator beinhaltete zahlreiche Objekte und Bilder, die verschiedene Heimateindrücke widerspiegeln und zuvor in einer „Feldforschung" zusammengetragen wurden. Über einen QR-Code und das eigene Smartphone konnten Passanten den Generator bedienen und mit den beinhalteten Heimatbildern bespielen. Output des Automaten waren individualisierte Heimat-Collagen mit überraschenden Kombinationen und Montagen, die ebenso widersprüchliche Impulse gaben wie der Begriff selbst. Betrachter konnten in Heimatstereotypen schwelgen und gleichzeitig die eigene Herkunft reflektieren. Die Installation lud, ohne den Zeigefinger zu erheben, spielerisch dazu ein, das eigene Verständnis von Heimat zu hinterfragen.

"Homeland" is a word that is currently discussed widely, but on closer consideration it is difficult to grasp. To stimulate a playful discussion about the meaning and multilayered nature of our concept of homeland, Atelier Markgraph developed the so-called homeland generator – a machine whose visual appearance already plays with German clichés. The generator, which evokes a cuckoo clock, contained numerous objects and pictures that reflect various homeland impressions and were gathered previously during "field research". Using a QR code and their own smartphone, passers-by could operate the generator and display the contained homeland images. The output of the machine were individualised homeland collages with surprising combinations and montages, which gave impulses as contradictory as the notion itself. Viewers could wallow in homeland stereotypes and at the same time reflect on their own origins. Without pointing a finger, the installation invited viewers playfully to question their own understanding of homeland.

ISPO MUNICH – HALL CONCEPT
ARNO DESIGN GMBH, MUNICH

Location
Messe München, Munich

Client
Messe München GmbH – ISPO Munich,
Munich

Month / Year
February 2017

Duration
several days

**Direction / Coordination / Architecture /
Design**
ARNO Design GmbH, Munich

Graphics
Klebebande, Berlin (Tape art); Bob Ross Inc.,
Sterling (Pictures)

Media / Films
Messe München GmbH – ISPO Munich

Artists / Show acts
Stephan Kaussner, Munich; Stefanie Raschke,
Munich; Peter Becker aka VJ Autopilot,
Munich; DJ Taliska, Munich; DJ Ales,
Munich; DJ Hot, Munich; VJ Serendipity,
Munich; PUBLIC POSSESSION DJs, Munich;
VJ Heiligenblut, Munich; TAM TAM -
Künstlernetzwerk, Munich; Ivan Saavedra,
Sofia; Herzstich, Munich; Patrick Hartl,
Munich; Kevin Ldk., Berlin; Michel H.,
Munich; Michal Ghaffar, Burma

Decoration
Im Raum Konzepte – Angelika Ann-Marie
Grupp, Munich

Catering
Able Catering GbR, Munich

Realisation
Stageco Deutschland GmbH, Berlin; Manert
Messebau & Service, Dusseldorf; Hoffmann
Messebau GmbH, Dusseldorf; Schreinerei
Grundner GmbH, St. Wolfgang

Others
BEKRA Hydrokulturen Vertriebs-GmbH,
Taufkirchen (Plants, greenery)

Photos
Ben Grna, Auerbach

Für die ISPO 2017 konzipierte und realisierte ARNO Design das Hallenkonzept der thematisch fokussierten Wintersport-Messe. Herzstück der Halle war der Mittelgang, der mit vier Bereichen und interaktiven Programmpunkten den räumlichen Treffpunkt bildete. Ziel und Herausforderung war es, über verschiedene Sonderflächen hinweg den Spirit der Winterbranche zu vereinen, ihn erlebbar und greifbar zu machen. Das Ergebnis war eine maßvolle, jedoch ausdrucksstarke Raumgestaltung, die der Weitläufigkeit der Location Struktur und eine urban-sportliche Atmosphäre verlieh.

EIN RAUMBILDENDES, STRUKTURIERENDES EVENTDESIGN MACHT DEN LIFESTYLE DER WINTERBRANCHE ERLEBBAR.

A SPACE-DEFINING AND STRUCTURING EVENT DESIGN MAKES IT POSSIBLE TO EXPERIENCE THE LIFESTYLE OF THE WINTER SPORTS SECTOR.

For ISPO 2017, ARNO Design designed and realised the hall concept of the thematically dense winter sports exhibition. The centrepiece of the hall was the central aisle, which formed the spatial hub with four areas and interactive programme points. The aim and the challenge were to summarise the spirit of the winter sports sector and to make it a tangible experience across various special areas. The result was a modest, but very expressive spatial design that structured the extensive location and gave it an urban-sporty atmosphere.

Die Community Loungebar lockte Besucher mit einer bunten, jungen Farbgestaltung aus Neon-Tape-Art sowie wechselnden Lichtstimmungen. Die Fläche diente als bewirtetes Restaurant und Besprechungsfläche für Aussteller und Besucher. Eine Sonderfläche im Bob-Ross-Stil verband die Wurzeln des Snowboardens mit dem bekannten Maler von Winterlandschaften. Original Bob-Ross-Bilder wurden auf Leinen gedruckt und über Holzbretter gespannt. Die im Industriecharme gehaltene Influencer Clublounge bot Bloggern und Influencern die Möglichkeit, live über Sport-Neuheiten zu berichten und Interviews zu führen. Akustisch wurde die Lounge-Atmosphäre durch bekannte DJs unterstützt. In der sogenannten Monochrom City gaben die Künstler Kevin LdK., Michel H. und Michal Ghaffar Einblick in ihre Kunst und Arbeitsweisen. Besucher konnten gemeinsam mit den Künstlern eigene Ideen realisieren sowie ein besonderes Andenken „mitnehmen": ein kostenfreies Tattoo von einem professionellen Tätowierer.

The Community Lounge Bar enticed visitors with a vibrant, youthful colour design made of neon tape art and changing lighting atmospheres. The area served as a restaurant and as a discussion forum for exhibitors and visitors. A special area in a Bob Ross style linked the roots of snowboarding with the well-known painter of winter landscapes. Original Bob Ross paintings were printed on cloth and stretched over wooden boards. The Influencer Club Lounge, featuring an industrial charm, offered bloggers and influencers the possibility to report live about sports news and to conduct interviews. The lounge atmosphere was enhanced acoustically by well-known DJs. In the "Monochrome City", the artists Kevin LdK., Michel H. and Michal Ghaffar provided insights into their art and ways of working. Visitors could realize their own ideas, together with the artists, and take away a special souvenir: a free tattoo by a professional tattoo artist.

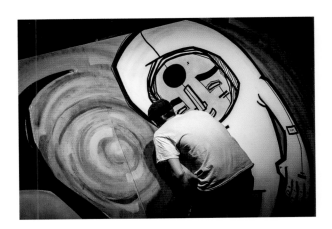

UNEXPECTED OPENING
DICOM EVENTS, BARCELONA

Location
Shopping Center Glories, Barcelona

Client
Unibail-Rodamco, Barcelona

Month / Year
November 2017

Duration
1 day

Photos
DICOM EVENTS, Barcelona

Die Aufmerksamkeit der Menschen zu gewinnen, ist heutzutage keine leichte Aufgabe. Das Unterhaltungsangebot ist groß, ebenso wie die Erwartungen der Menschen. Um die Neueröffnung und Neupositionierung der Shopping-Mall Glories in Barcelona stadtweit bekannt zu machen, hat Dicom Events genau aus diesem Grund groß gedacht. Die Wiedereröffnung wurde zu einem überraschenden, bombastischen Großevent – einem Unexpected Opening. Schon im Vorfeld sollte die Neugier durch verschiedene Online-, Radio- und Promotion-Aktionen geweckt werden. Ein „Heer" aus Models machte an den bedeutendsten Orten der Stadt auf das Event aufmerksam. Ein eigens entworfener Mantel diente als Wiedererkennungsmerkmal der gesamten Kampagne. Video- und AV Teaser wurden in verschiedenen Medien platziert.

It is no easy task nowadays to attract people's attention. The range of entertainment on offer is so great, as well as people's expectations. To publicise the reopening and repositioning of the Glories shopping centre in Barcelona throughout the city, Dicom Events thought in terms of greatness for precisely this reason. The reopening turned into a surprising, bombastic major event, an Unexpected Opening. Curiosity was awakened in advance through various online, radio and promotion activities. An "army" of models drew attention to the event in the most prominent areas of the city. A specially designed coat served as a recognition feature of the whole campaign. Video and AV teasers were placed in a variety of media.

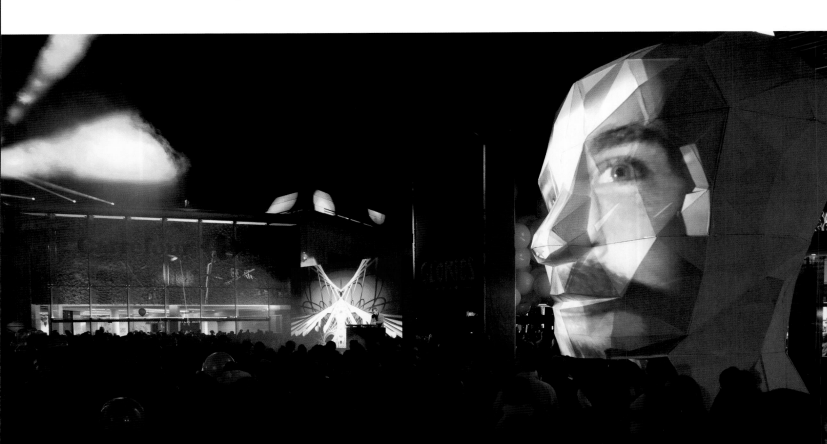

FULMINANTE PERFORMANCES UND SKULPTUREN MACHEN AUS EINER SHOPPING-MALL-WIEDERERÖFFNUNG EIN STADTBEKANNTES EVENTSPEKTAKEL.

Nach einer solch aufwendigen Einladung sollten die 61.000 Besucher am Eröffnungstag nicht enttäuscht werden. Eigens kreierte künstlerische Performances, namhafte DJs und Moderatoren, überdimensionale interaktive Skulpturen und nicht zuletzt ein Feuerwerk machten die Eröffnung zu einem fulminanten Erlebnis. Zusammen mit dem Künstler Franc Aleu wurde eine Performance aus Musik, interaktivem Tanz auf den Gebäuden der Mall sowie einer energiegeladenen Percussion-Lichtshow entwickelt. Eine sieben Meter hohe Skulptur in Form eines Kopfes diente als dreidimensionale Projektionsfläche, auf der Besucher ihre Gesichter projizieren lassen konnten. Zur großen Überraschung wurde der Kopf erneut, als er sich im Verlauf des Events als DJ-Kabine entpuppte. In Summe erzeugte das Event 100.000 Video-Views, 47 Millionen Impressions auf Facebook und einen PR-Wert von 609.000 Euro.

After such an elaborate invitation, the 61,000 visitors on the opening day were scarcely disappointed. Specially created artistic performances, renowned DJs and presenters, large-scale interactive sculptures and not least fireworks made the opening event a fulminant experience. Together with the artist Franc Aleu, a performance comprising music, interactive dance on the mall buildings and an energy-laden percussion and light show was developed. A seven-metre-high sculpture in the form of a head served as a three-dimensional projection surface, which the visitors could project their faces onto. The head became a surprising feature once again when it emerged as a DJ cubicle over the course of the event. In total, the event generated 100,000 video views, 47 impressions on Facebook and a PR value of 609,000 euros.

FULMINANT PERFORMANCES AND SCULPTURES TURN A SHOPPING CENTRE REOPENING INTO AN EVENT SPECTACLE THAT DREW ATTENTION THROUGHOUT THE CITY.

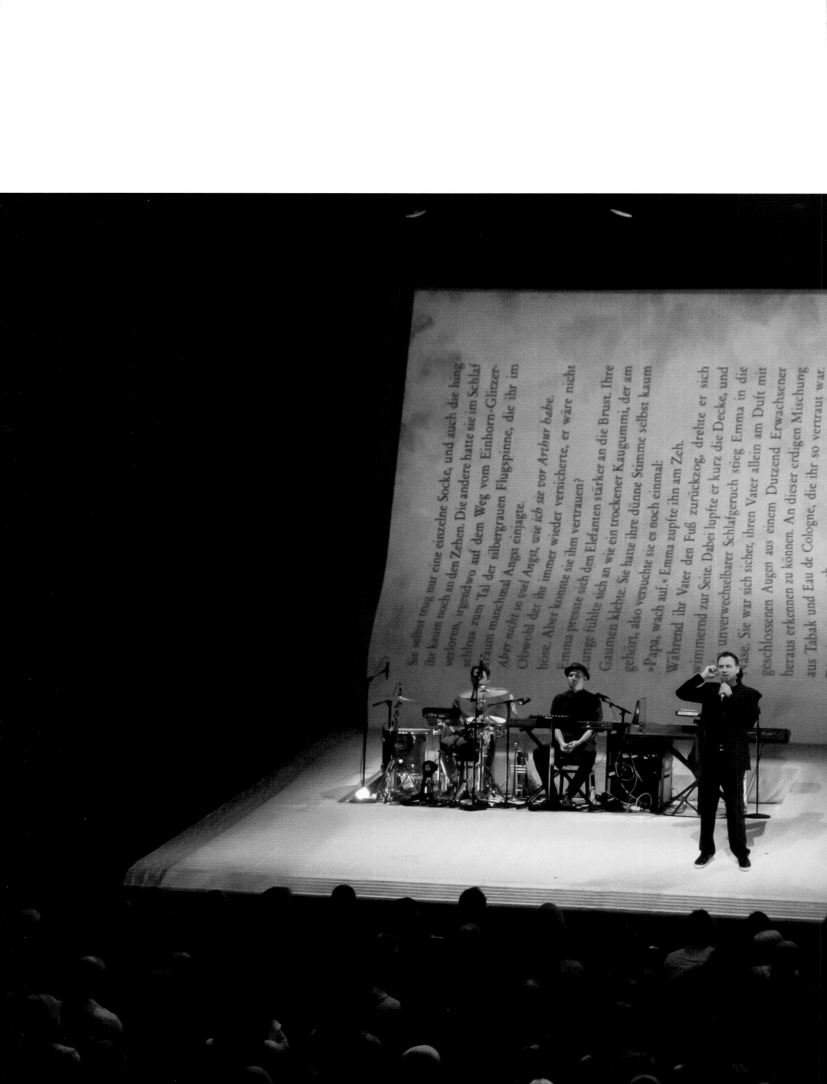

„10 JAHRE FITZEK" ANNIVERSARY SHOW
PXNG.LI GMBH, KARLSRUHE; VALENTIN LÜDICKE, HEIDELBERG; PERIPHERIQUE PQ-WORLD GMBH, BAD KÖNIG

Location
several cities, Austria / Germany / Switzerland

Client
Peripherique pq-world GmbH, Bad König

Month / Year
October – November 2016

Duration
several weeks

Dramaturgy / Graphics
Peripherique pq-world GmbH; PXNG.LI GmbH, Karlsruhe

Direction / Coordination
Sebastian Fitzek, Berlin; Peripherique pq-world GmbH; PXNG.LI GmbH

Architecture / Design
Valentin Lüdicke, Heidelberg; Peripherique pq-world GmbH; PXNG.LI GmbH

Lighting
Valentin Lüdicke

Media / Films
PXNG.LI GmbH

Music
Buffer Underrun, Berlin

Artists / Show acts
Sebastian Fitzek

Realisation
Peripherique pq-world GmbH

Photos
PXNG.LI GmbH, Karlsruhe

Ende 2016 ging der deutsche „Meister des Psycho-Thrillers", Sebastian Fitzek, auf eine Lesetour der besonderen Art. Zusammen mit der „10 Jahre Fitzek Jubiläumstour" erschien sein neues Buch *Das Paket*. Beide Anlässe sollten mit einer Reihe besonderer Lesungen gemeinsam gefeiert werden. PXNG.LI gestaltete für diesen Rahmen eine auf den Inhalt abgestimmte Bühnenprojektion. Zusammen mit der Band Buffer Underrun wurden die Lesungen visuell und musikalisch begleitet – eine für diese Art von Veranstaltungen unkonventionelle Kombination aus Lesung, Live-Musik und Mapping-Projektionen.

At the end of 2016, the German "master of the psycho-thriller" Sebastian Fitzek went on a special kind of reading tour. At the same time as the "10 years Fitzek anniversary tour", his new book *Das Paket* ('The Package') was published. Both occasions were to be celebrated together by means of a series of special readings. PXNG.LI designed a stage projection for this purpose that related to the content. In cooperation with the band Buffer Underrun, the readings were accompanied visually and musically – a combination of reading, the band and mapping projections that is unconventional for this type of event.

LIVE-MUSIK, MAPPING-PROJEKTIONEN UND EFFEKTVOLLES BÜHNENDESIGN MACHEN EINE LESE-TOUR ZUR AUSSER-GEWÖHNLICHEN SHOW.

Das eng aufeinander abgestimmte visuelle Konzept aus Bühne, Licht und Video wurde von Valentin Lüdicke und Dominik Rinnhofer entwickelt. Für jedes Kapitel wurden speziell gestaltete Projektionen und Impressionen umgesetzt, die Hintergrund, Boden und Lesepult bespielten. Stimmungsvolle Szenen aus im Buch beschriebenen Kulissen untermalten die Lesung und beflügelten die Fantasie der Zuschauer. Die Bühnengestaltung mit Backdrop-Leinwand und leicht schrägem Boden erweckte den effektvollen Eindruck eines überdimensional großen, aufgeklappten Buches. Eingebettet in das Bühnendesign erhielten die Musiker einen prominenten und gestalterisch stimmigen Platz. Mit Rücksicht auf einen effizienten Transport während der Jubiläumstour wurden Bühne und Leinwand tourtauglich aus Holz gebaut.

The coherently harmonised visual concept composed of the stage, light and video was developed by Valentin Lüdicke and Dominik Rinnhofer. Specially designed projections and impressions were realised for each chapter, playing out on the background, floor and lectern. Atmospheric scenes from settings described in the book accompanied the reading and sparked the imagination of the viewers. The stage design with a backdrop screen and a slightly sloping floor created the impression of an oversized open book. The musicians were given a prominent and atmospherically designed place, nestled into the stage design. The stage and screen were made of wood, in the interests of efficient transport during the anniversary tour.

LIVE MUSIC, MAPPING PROJECTIONS AND A STRIKING STAGE DESIGN TURN A READING TOUR INTO AN EXCEPTIONAL SHOW.

„ERLEBNIS STAHL" BEI DER NACHT DER INDUSTRIEKULTUR
FLUUR – BÜRO FÜR INTERAKTIVE GESTALTUNG, COLOGNE

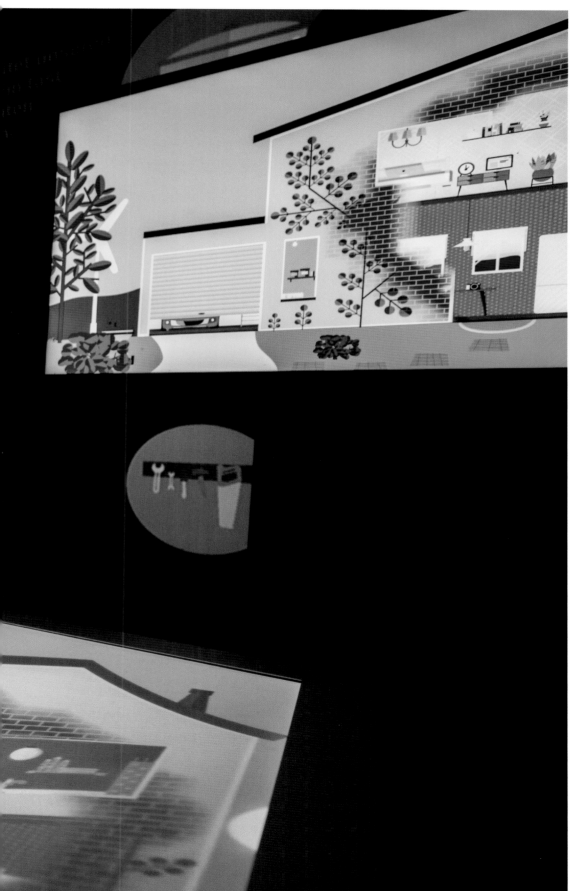

Location
thyssenkrupp Steel Europe AG, Duisburg

Client
thyssenkrupp Steel Europe AG

Month / Year
June 2016

Duration
several days

Dramaturgy / Direction / Coordination
37 Grad Büro für Live-Kommunikation GmbH, Cologne

Graphics / Development
FLUUR – Büro for interaktive Gestaltung, Cologne

Audio-visual technology
CST Cologne Sound Technologies GmbH, Cologne

Realisation
Stella | Raum und Möbelgestaltung, Cologne

Photos
Christoph Stallkamp, Cologne

EIN HAPTISCH-DIGI-TALES ERLEBNIS LÄDT ZUM INTERAKTIVEN ENTDECKEN VON STAHL IN ALLTAGS-PRODUKTEN EIN.

Seit 2001 setzt das Kulturfestival „ExtraSchicht" die Metropole Ruhr und ihr industriekulturelles Erbe in Szene. Als Nacht der Industriekultur bespielen jährlich rund 2.000 Künstler ehemalige Industrieanlagen, Museen sowie Landmarken und ziehen bis zu 200.000 Besucher an. Die thyssenkrupp Steel Europe AG öffnete zu diesem Anlass die Pforten ihres Duisburger Werksgeländes. Unter dem Titel „Erlebnis Stahl" gewährte der Konzern Einblicke in die Stahlproduktion und vermittelte unter anderem, in wie vielen Alltagsprodukten Stahl zu finden ist.

Since 2001, the "ExtraSchicht" cultural festival has been casting a spotlight on the metropolitan Ruhr and its industrial and cultural heritage. During the Night of Industrial Culture, every year around 2000 artists animate former industrial sites, museums and landmarks and draw up to 200,000 visitors. On this occasion, thyssenkrupp Steel Europe AG opened the gates to its Duisburg factory premises. Under the title "Erlebnis Stahl" (Experience steel), the corporation granted insights into steel production and conveyed, amongst other things, in how many everyday products steel can be found.

A HAPTIC-DIGITAL EXPERIENCE INVITES VISITORS TO INTERACTIVELY EXPLORE STEEL IN EVERYDAY PRODUCTS.

Mithilfe des 3D-Multitouchtisches „Kreek" konnten Besucher buchstäblich durch die Fassaden von Einfamilienhäusern blicken und entdecken, wie häufig sie mit Stahl in Berührung kommen. Eine elastische Projektionsfläche ermöglichte es, unter der Verwendung von Druck unterschiedliche Objekte oder Ebenen anzusteuern. Je tiefer man die Projektionsfläche eindrückte, desto mehr zuvor unsichtbare Ebenen öffneten sich und gewährten einen Blick in das Innere von beispielsweise Häusern, PKWs oder Laptops. Die physische Interaktion mit dem elastischen Projektionsstoff lud zum Entdecken ein und ließ ein symbiotisches Erlebnis aus digitalen und haptischen Elementen entstehen. Komplettiert wurde die explorative Anwendung durch zwei Flatscreens, auf denen weitere Hintergrundinformationen über die Produktentwicklung und Fachkompetenz von thyssenkrupp Steel kommuniziert wurden.

With the help of the 3D multitouch table "Kreek", visitors were literally able to look through the façades of single-family houses and discover how often they came into contact with steel. An elastic projection surface allowed them to home in on different objects or floors by pressing it. The deeper one pressed the projection surface in, the more previously unseen levels opened up and afforded a view into the interior of e.g. houses, cars or laptops. The physical interaction with the elastic projection fabric invited one to explore and created a symbiotic experience with digital and haptic elements. The explorative application was completed by two flatscreens, which communicated additional background information about product development and the specialist competence of thyssenkrupp Steel.

AUDI BERLINALE LOUNGE
PLANWERKSTATT GMBH, BEDBURG-HAU

Location
Marlene-Dietrich-Platz, Berlin

Client
AUDI AG, Ingolstadt

Month / Year
February 2017

Duration
several days

Direction / Coordination
AUDI AG

Architecture / Design / Graphics / Decoration
Planwerkstatt GmbH, Bedburg-Hau

Lighting
macomNIYU GmbH, Berlin

Media
Pacific Entertainment Media GmbH,
Munich; envy GmbH, Frankfurt a. Main

Films / Artists / Show acts
Pacific Entertainment Media GmbH

Catering
Grand Hyatt Berlin, Berlin

Realisation
A&A Messe- und Ausstellungsbau GmbH,
Dusseldorf; Gorges tent-event, Laubach

Others
lmc.communication GmbH, Stuttgart
(Hospitality Management)

Photos
Getty für Audi

Well-known events are an ideal starting point for experience-oriented marketing activities. They allow one to reach not only a wide public, many media representatives and perhaps celebrities, but also quite specific target groups, such as at the Berlinale, the largest German film festival. In 2017, Audi made use of this framework to present itself as a company oriented towards creativity – both on site with the Audi Lounge and theme-specific content, as well as online with the help of influencers who reported live from the film festival.

Bekannte Veranstaltungen sind ein idealer Anknüpfungspunkt für erlebnisorientierte Marketingaktivitäten. Auf diesem Wege lassen sich nicht nur eine große Öffentlichkeit, viele Medienvertreter und gegebenenfalls Prominente, sondern auch ganz bestimmte Zielgruppen erreichen; so auch auf der Berlinale, den größten deutschen Filmfestspielen. Diesen Rahmen nutzte Audi 2017, um sich als der Kreativität zugewandtes Unternehmen zu präsentieren – vor Ort mit der Audi Lounge und themenspezifischen Inhalten sowie online mithilfe von Influencern, die live von den Filmfestspielen berichteten.

THE PROXIMITY TO THE FILM INDUSTRY IS USED AS A BRAND TOUCHPOINT AND AS A PLATFORM FOR THE TOPIC OF AUTONOMOUS DRIVING.

Die zweigeschossige Audi Lounge lag als separater Pavillon direkt am Roten Teppich und in unmittelbarer Nähe zu den Stars und Sternchen der Filmbranche. Der futuristisch anmutende Bau bot Besuchern verschiedene Angebote rund um das Thema Kino. Hier konnten Diskussions- und Fragerunden mit den Teams der Wettbewerbsfilme verfolgt und die Schnittstellen zwischen der Film- und Automobilindustrie entdeckt werden. Audi nutzte außerdem den Kontext und das Medium Film, um das Thema „Autonomes Fahren" vorzustellen. Aufwändig produzierte Kurzfilme zeigten, wie Prominente – zum Beispiel Schauspieler Clemens Schick – von künstlichen Filmcharakteren (Johnny Cab, „Total Recall") in autonom fahrenden Fahrzeugen zum Festspielhaus chauffiert werden. Nicht zuletzt diente die Lounge zum Verweilen, Entspannen und – bei der Berlinale Lounge Night – zum Feiern. Auf der XXL-Social-Wall wurde live übertragen, was Influencer auf der Berlinale erlebten und im Internet berichteten.

DIE NÄHE ZUR FILMBRANCHE WIRD ALS MARKEN-TOUCHPOINT UND PLATTFORM FÜR DAS THEMA AUTONOMES FAHREN GENUTZT.

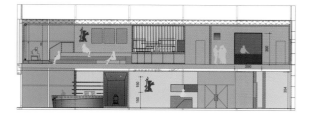

The two-storey Audi Lounge stood as a separate pavilion right by the Red Carpet and very close to the stars and starlets of the film industry. The building with a futuristic flair offered visitors a varied program surrounding the theme of cinema. Discussion and question rounds could be pursued with the teams from the competing movies and cross-over points could be discovered between the film and car industries. Audi also used the context and the medium of film to present the topic of autonomous driving. Elaborately produced short movies showed how celebrities – for example the actor Clemens Schick – were chauffeured to the festival venue by virtual movie characters (Johnny Cab, "Total Recall") in autonomously driving vehicles. Not least, the lounge served as a place to call in, relax and – on the Berlinale Lounge Night – to celebrate. The XXL social wall transmitted live what influencers were experiencing at the Berlinale and reporting on the Internet.

LIGHT MATTERS
ACTLD, BRUSSELS

Location
Jonas Daniel Meijerplein, Amsterdam

Client
Amsterdam Light Festival, Amsterdam

Month / Year
November 2017 – January 2018

Duration
several months

**Dramaturgy / Direction / Coordination /
Architecture / Design / Graphics / Music**
ACTLD, Brussels

Realisation
Amsterdam Light Festival

Photos
Janus van den Eijnden, Amsterdam

Seit Anbeginn der Zeit sorgt natürliches Licht für Wachstum, Wohlergehen und faszinierende, wundersame Effekte. Künstliche Lichtquellen, die das heutige menschliche Umfeld nahezu durchgehend erhellen, nehmen vielen dieser Phänomene die Grundlage. Seltene Schätze natürlichen Lichts verstecken sich heute nur noch an Orten der absoluten Dunkelheit. So gerät gleichzeitig in Vergessenheit, dass Licht eine lange vor dem Menschen existierende physikalische Größe von enormer Wichtigkeit ist. Um diese Bedeutung und den Existenzialismus von Licht zu illustrieren, entwickelte ACTLD eine außergewöhnliche Medieninstallation, die im Rahmen des Amsterdamer Light Festivals 2017 / 2018 zu sehen war.

FLOATING PROJECTIONS ILLUSTRATE THE EXISTENTIALISM OF LIGHT WITH FASCINATING, NATURAL LIGHT PHENOMENA.

SCHWEBENDE PROJEKTIONEN ILLUSTRIEREN MIT FASZINIERENDEN, NATÜRLICHEN LICHT-PHÄNOMENEN DEN EXISTENZIALISMUS VON LICHT.

Since the beginning of time, natural light has provided growth and well-being, as well as fascinating, wondrous effects. Artificial light sources, which illuminate the present-day human environment almost continuously, preclude many of these phenomena. Rare gems of natural light are only concealed today in places of absolute darkness. At the same time, it is being forgotten that light has a longstanding physical significance that existed before humans and is of enormous importance. To illustrate this significance and the existentialism of light, ACTLD developed an exceptional media installation that was shown as part of the Amsterdam Light Festival 2017/2018.

Die Installation „Light Matters" inszenierte eine Reise um die Welt auf Entdeckung natürlicher Phänomene, die sich wie Diamanten in einer Grube verstecken. Nach Einbruch der Dunkelheit erschienen fließende, farbenfrohe Lichter zwischen den Bäumen und bespielten den städtischen Nachthimmel. Eine unsichtbare Projektionsoberfläche fing faszinierende natürliche Szenen aus Lichtern, Farben und Formen ein und ließ eine magische Lichtwolke entstehen, die über den Köpfen der Besucher schwebte. Untermalt von Klängen konnten sich die Betrachter während einer Fahrt auf dem Kanal, einem Besuch des Jonas Daniël Meijerplein Parks oder auf dem Fußweg verzaubern lassen. Light Matters brachte einzigartige vergessene Lichtphänomene in die Stadt und illustrierte die faszinierende Wandlungsfähigkeit, Kraft und Schönheit von Licht, das so viel älter als ist der Mensch.

The installation "Light Matters" staged a journey around the world, to discover these natural phenomena that are hiding like diamonds in a mine. At nightfall, flowing and colourful lights appeared between the trees and played on the urban night sky. An invisible projection surface captured fascinating, natural scenes with lights, colours and shapes and created a magical light cloud that floated above the heads of visitors. Accompanied by sounds, the viewers could immerse themselves in the magic during a ride on the canal, a visit to the Jonas Daniël Meijerplein Park or along footpaths. Light Matters brought unique, forgotten light phenomena to the city and illustrated the mesmerising versatility, power and beauty of light, which has been around so much longer than man.

MELITTA FESTIVALTOUR
EAST END COMMUNICATIONS GMBH, HAMBURG

Location
Rock am Ring, Nürburg; Hurricane, Scheeßel;
Lollapalooza Berlin, Berlin

Client
Melitta Europa GmbH & Co. KG, Bremen

Month / Year
June – September 2017

Duration
several days

**Direction / Coordination / Architecture /
Design / Graphics**
EAST END COMMUNICATIONS GmbH,
Hamburg

Catering
Melitta Europa GmbH & Co. KG

Realisation
Artlife GmbH, Hofheim

Photos
alinea.design, Hamburg

Auch der energischste Festivalbesucher braucht einmal eine Kaffeepause – idealerweise in einem gemütlichen Wohnzimmer mit WLAN und Strom für das Smartphone – kurzum im Festival-Wohnzimmer der Marke Melitta. Unter dem Motto „Friede, Freude, Beats & Bohne" entwickelte EAST END ein 250 Quadratmeter großes und zweistöckiges Wohnzimmer. Mit einem Mix aus Vintage-Elementen und modernen Möbeln präsentierte sich die Kaffeemarke auf den Campsites der Musikfestivals Rock am Ring und Hurricane sowie auf dem Lollapalooza Berlin. Ziel war es, auf lässige und sympathische Art und Weise in Erscheinung zu treten und mit den Festivalbesuchern in Kontakt zu kommen.

EINE ENTSPANNTE KAFFEEAUSZEIT IN LÄSSIGER WOHNZIMMER-ATMOSPHÄRE – SO KOMMT MELITTA MIT FESTIVALBESUCHERN IN KONTAKT.

Even the most energetic festival visitor occasionally needs a coffee break – ideally in a cosy lounge with Wi-Fi and electricity for recharging the smartphone, in summary the festival lounge of the Melitta brand. According to the motto "Friede, Freude, Beats & Bohne" (Peace, Joy, Beats & Beans), EAST END developed a 250-square-metre two-storey lounge. The coffee brand presented itself at the sites of the music festivals Rock am Ring and Hurricane as well as at the Lollapalooza Berlin with a mix of vintage elements and modern furniture. The aim was to have a casual and friendly presence and to establish contact with the festival visitors.

A RELAXING COFFEE BREAK IN A CASUAL LOUNGE ATMOSPHERE – THIS IS HOW MELITTA MADE CONTACT WITH FESTIVAL VISITORS.

OBERGESCHOSS

ERDGESCHOSS

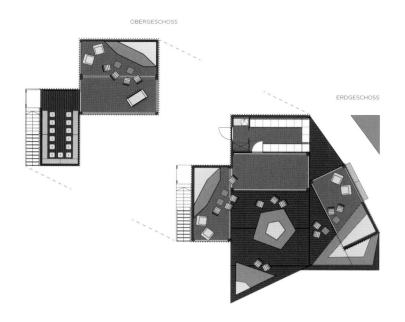

On the ground floor, an open and homely style with wall-papered walls, pictures and photographs invited visitors to enjoy a leisurely coffee break. The rooftop terrace with greenery on the upper floor offered a perfect overview over the site. Visual highlights included the modular wooden façade with a slatted veneer, as well as the seven-metre-high coffee mill that presented visitors with a strong brand signal already from afar. For the visitors on site, the festival lounge also offered an ideal selfie setting, not least owing to Wi-Fi and the fully recharged mobile phone battery. Additional coffee bars built in the same style were positioned in the infield and allowed a coffee break between the music acts. The Melitta festival tour received media support through bloggers and YouTubers who provided their online fans and followers with updates on the tour throughout the summer.

Im Erdgeschoss lud ein offener, wohnlicher Stil mit tapezierten Wänden, Bildern und Fotografien zur gemütlichen Kaffeepause ein. Die begrünte Dachterrasse im Obergeschoss bot den perfekten Überblick über das Gelände. Optische Highlights waren die modulare Holzfassade in Lamellenoptik sowie die in sieben Meter Höhe befindliche Kaffeemühle, die den Besuchern schon von Weitem ein starkes Markensignal zeigte. Für die Besucher vor Ort bot das Festival-Wohnzimmer wiederum die ideale Selfie-Kulisse, nicht zuletzt dank WLAN und dem wieder voll aufgeladenen Handy-Akku. Ergänzende, im gleichen Stil gebaute Coffee-Bars wurden im Infield platziert und ermöglichten eine Kaffeeauszeit zwischen den Music-Acts. Mediale Unterstützung bekam die Melitta Festivaltour durch Influencer wie Blogger und YouTuber, die über den Sommer hinweg ihre Online-Fans und -Follower mit Updates zur Tour versorgten.

OPENING CEREMONY
OF EXPO ASTANA
STARPROJECT LLC, MOSCOW;
ADHOC ENGINEERING GMBH, POTSDAM;
ANDREE VERLEGER, KERPEN

Location
Congress Hall, Astana

Client
JSC "National Company "Astana EXPO-2017",
Astana

Month / Year
June 2017

Duration
1 day

Dramaturgy
Andree Verleger, Kerpen

Direction
Vyacheslav Kulayev, Moscow

Production
Borislav Volodin, Moscow

Agency / Coordination
StarProject LLC, Moscow

Technical Production
Tarmo Krimm, Tallin

Technical Planning / Technical Direction
adhoc engineering GmbH, Potsdam

Lighting Design
Jerry Appelt Licht Design, Hamburg

Media
Raketamedia, Moscow; N3 Design, Moscow

Music
Aleksandr Knyazev, Moscow

Technology
PRG, Hamburg (Lighting / Video); Live
Sound Agency, Moscow (Audio); Stage
Kinetik GmbH, Castrop-Rauxel (Kinetics);
Airstage, Schlaitdorf (Airorb); DreamLaser,
Moscow (Black trax)

Decoration
Fabrika Art, Moscow

Realisation
MF Group, Moscow

Photos
Olli Waldhauer, Berlin

Die Expo 2017 in Astana, Kasachstan, stand unter dem Thema „Future Energy". Ebenso wie die Weltausstellung sollte die Opening Ceremony den Aufbruch in die komplexe Welt der zukünftigen Energie und Nachhaltigkeit inszenieren. Inhaltlich galt es die wesentlichen, natürlichen Ressourcen in kraftvollen, spannungsreichen Bildern und einer abwechslungsreichen Show zu arrangieren. Die Kernidee der Inszenierung war es, Energie als ursprüngliches Phänomen der Natur zu zeigen, das alles um sich herum durchdringt: Natur, Mensch und Energie sind zu einer Einheit miteinander verbunden. Andree Verleger und adhoc gestalteten dafür in Kooperation mit StarProject eine technisch ausgefeilte, dreidimensionale mediale Szenografie. Videoprojektionen, kinetische Installationen und Performances nutzten das komplette Volumen des Setdesigns, um die Betrachter in faszinierende Bilder abtauchen zu lassen. Die Form der Darstellung sollte Referenz für das komplexe Thema „Zukunft" sein und gleichzeitig eine neuartige Gestaltung von Inhalten ermöglichen.

Expo 2017 in Astana, Kazakhstan, was led by the topic of "Future Energy". Just like the world exhibition, the Opening Ceremony was designed to stage the departure into the complex world of future energy and sustainability. In terms of content, it was about representing the relevant natural resources in powerful and exciting images and a varied show. The main idea of the production was to show Energy as a primordial phenomena of nature pervading everything around: Nature, Human and Energy are linked as unity. Andree Verleger and adhoc in cooperation with StarProject designed a technically sophisticated, three-dimensional media scenography for this purpose. Video projections, kinetic installations and performances used the full volume of the set design to immerse viewers in fascinating images. The presentation form was intended as a reference to the complex subject of "future" and at the same time to enable a novel content design.

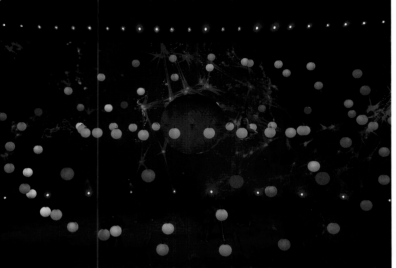

EINE TECHNISCH AUFWÄNDIGE UND FULMINANTE INSZENIERUNG ALS REFERENZ FÜR DAS KOMPLEXE THEMA „ZUKUNFT".

Eine Vielzahl technischer Elemente schuf die Grundlage für diese fulminante Inszenierung. Neben einer 180°-Horizontprojektion wurde eine Bodenprojektion als wandelbares Bühnenbild eingesetzt. Für die dreidimensionalen Effekte wurden drei transparente Gazeleinwände zwischen der Bühne und dem Publikum angebracht. Drohnen, die autonom auf vorprogrammierten Flugbahnen flogen, wurden mittels Videotracking mit Content bespielt. Ergänzend zu den Tänzern auf der Bühne schwebten Tänzerinnen an Horizontalwinden zwischen einem Meer aus circa 400 kinetischen LED-Bällen. Neben den technischen und inhaltlichen Herausforderungen war auch das Zusammenspiel der vielen internationalen Beteiligten, u. a. aus Kasachstan, Russland, Deutschland und dem Baltikum, eine erwähnenswerte Aufgabe.

A range of technical elements created the basis for this fulminant staging. Apart from a 180° horizon projection, a floor projection was used as a variable stage set. Three transparent gauze screens were set up between the stage and the public for the three-dimensional effects. Drones that flew on programmed flight paths were animated with content by means of video tracking. Accompanying the dancers on the stage, dancers drifted on horizontal winches amidst a sea of around 400 kinetic LED balls. Apart from the technical and content challenges, a further notable task was the interplay of the wide international cast, including from Kazakhstan, Germany and the Baltic States.

A TECHNICALLY SOPHISTICATED AND FULMINANT STAGING AS A REFERENCE FOR THE COMPLEX TOPIC OF THE FUTURE.

Jede Zielgruppe hat unterschiedliche Bedürfnisse und Erwartungen. Dementsprechend sind Eventkonzepte im Idealfall nicht nur auf den Absender, sondern vor allem auf die Empfänger zugeschnitten.

CONSUMERS: VERBRAUCHER ODER KONSUMENTEN, DIE EINE ODER MEHRERE WAREN ODER DIENSTLEISTUNGEN ZUR EIGENEN (PRIVATEN) BEDÜRFNISBEFRIEDIGUNG KÄUFLICH ERWERBEN WOLLEN ODER VIELMEHR SOLLEN. DABEI HANDELT ES SICH MEIST UM NOCH UNBEKANNTE, ABER SCHON INTERESSIERTE PERSONEN, DIE ZU LANGJÄHRIGEN, TREUEN KUNDEN WERDEN KÖNNTEN UND DAMIT DER ABSATZFÖRDERUNG VON UNTERNEHMEN DIENEN.

Each target group has different requirements and expectations. Event concepts are therefore ideally not only geared towards the addressor, but especially towards the recipients.

CONSUMERS: CONSUMERS OR USERS ARE THOSE WHO WANT TO OR SHOULD PURCHASE ONE OR SEVERAL PRODUCTS OR SERVICES TO SATISFY THEIR OWN (PRIVATE) REQUIREMENTS. THEY ARE MOSTLY STILL UNKNOWN, BUT ALREADY INTERESTED PERSONS WHO COULD BECOME LONG-STANDING, LOYAL CUSTOMERS AND THEREFORE BENEFIT THE SALES PROMOTION OF THE COMPANY.

INFINIUM EVENT
DREINULL AGENTUR FÜR MEDIATAINMENT GMBH & CO. KG, BERLIN

Location
PVA Expo Praha, Prague

Month / Year
December 2017

Duration
1 day

Dramaturgy / Architecture / Design / Graphics
DREINULL Agentur für Mediatainment GmbH & Co. KG, Berlin; battleROYAL GmbH, Berlin

Direction / Coordination
DREINULL Agentur für Mediatainment GmbH & Co. KG; battleROYAL GmbH, Berlin

Lighting
AMBION GmbH, Berlin; Chris Moylan / Optikalusion, Berlin

Media
AMBION GmbH; DNM | DREINULLMOTION GmbH, Berlin

Music
AELI, Dubai; Omar Basaad, Dubai; Looptrigger, Berlin; Julian Laping, Berlin; Hara Katsiki, Berlin; Smack, Prague; Idiotape, Seoul; Booka Shade, Berlin; Claptone, Berlin; Oliver Koletzki, Berlin

Artists / Show acts
Les Enfants Terribles, London; battleROYAL GmbH

Decoration
BALLONI GmbH, Berlin, Cologne; WERKSTOFF, Berlin; Ludwig Jenssen, Berlin; Spot On, Prague; Floressenz, Berlin

Catering
Bompas & Parr, London; White Circus Catering, Prague

Others
Poetic Kinetics, Los Angeles (Set / Installations); Ralf Kollmann / mobilee records, Berlin (DJs / Line Up); Lunchmeat, Prague (DMC / Installations); LASA Berlin, Berlin (Installations); NAVITAS Solutions GmbH, Berlin (IT development); FLASH BARRANDOV Special Effects Ltd., Prague (Special effects)

Photos
Michal Adamovský, Prague; Marcus Zumbansen, Berlin

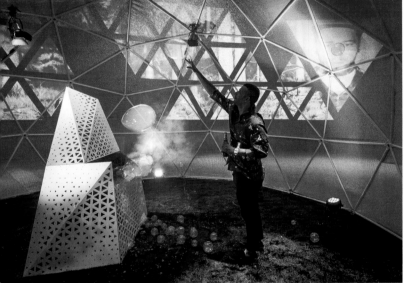

Wird im Rahmen von Events über eine individuelle Ausrichtung gesprochen, bezieht sich das in der Regel auf die Gruppe der angesprochenen Gäste. Jeder einzelne Gast erlebt jedoch zumeist das Gleiche und hat selten individuelle Auswahlmöglichkeiten. Anders war es bei einem spektakulären Party-Event in Prag. In Zusammenarbeit mit verschiedenen Künstlern entstand eine surreale Welt getreu dem Motto „choose your own adventure".

EIN „CHOOSE YOUR OWN ADVENTURE" SCHAFFT FÜR JEDEN EINZELNEN GAST INDIVIDUELLE ERLEBNISWELTEN.

If we speak about individual orientation in the context of events, it generally refers to the group of guests who are being appealed to. Each individual guest, however, usually experiences the same and rarely has any personal choice. It was quite different in the case of a spectacular party event in Prague. In cooperation with various artists, a surreal world was created in accordance with the motto "choose your own adventure".

THE PRINCIPLE OF "CHOOSE YOUR OWN ADVENTURE" CREATES INDIVIDUAL WORLDS OF EXPERIENCE FOR EVERY SINGLE GUEST.

Mit dem Ziel, verschiedene Facetten von Genuss in den Mittelpunkt zu stellen und zu feiern, realisierten DREINULL und battleROYAL eine fantastische Party- und Erlebniswelt. Die räumliche, musikalische und kulinarische Gestaltung stand unter der künstlerischen Ägide von Poetic Kinetics, den DJ-Stars AELI und Omar Basaad und den experimentierfreudigen Food-Avantgardisten Bompas & Parr. Inhaltlich entwickelte das Londoner Immersive Theatre Les Enfants Terribles eine narrative Klammer und erzählte aus einer Welt, in der drei Stämme nach dem richtigen Weg in die Zukunft strebten. So entstand ein Hybrid aus Immersive Theatre, interaktivem „choose your own adventure" und multimedialer Erlebniswelt. In rund 50 individuellen interaktiven Stationen konnte jeder Gast selbst wählen, was er als Nächstes erleben möchte. Unterschiedlich inszenierte Etappen ermöglichten jedem Besucher, eigene Erlebnisse jeweils selbst zusammenzustellen. Eine zentrale, für alle gemeinsame Inszenierung war das finale Highlight, bevor der Abend in einer fulminanten Party mündete.

With the goal of placing a focus on and celebrating various facets of enjoyment, DREINULL and battleROYAL realised an impressive party and world of experience. The spatial, musical and culinary design was under the artistic aegis of Poetic Kinetics, the star DJs AELI and Omar Basaad, and the experimental food avant-gardists Bompas & Parr. In terms of content, the London immersive theatre Les Enfants Terribles developed a narrative framework and told of a world in which three tribes are striving for the right way into the future. This resulted in a hybrid of immersive theatre, interactive "choose your own adventure" and a multimedia world of experience. At around 50 individual interactive stations, each guest could choose what to experience next. The variously staged stations allowed each visitor to put together their own experiences. The final highlight was a central display for everyone together, before the evening culminated in an fulminant party.

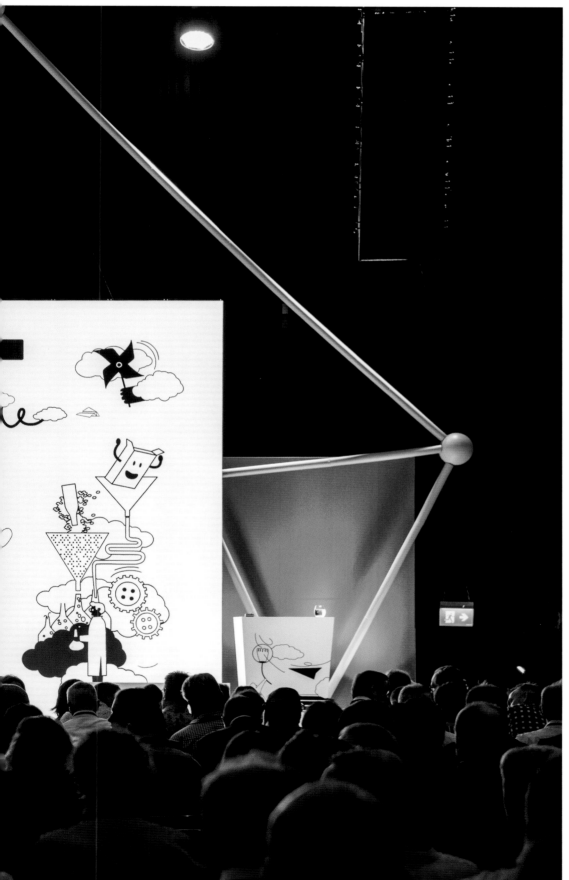

THINK NEXT BY FRANKE
RUFENER EVENTS, ZURICH

Location
Franke Headquarters, Aarburg

Client
Franke Management AG, Aarburg

Month / Year
August 2017

Duration
1 day

Concept / Dramaturgy / Direction / Coordination
Rufener Events, Zurich; Franke Management AG

Architecture / Design
Rufener Events; Oceansalt LLC, Zurich

Graphics
Rufener Events

Lighting
Winkler Livecom AG, Wohlen

Media
Farner Consulting AG, Zurich

Films
glimpses GmbH, Zurich

Music
David Suivez, Zurich (DJ); The Phly Boyz, Nice; Tim und Puma Mimi, Zurich

Artists / Show acts
Bruno Barbieri, Reggio Emilia; René Schudel, Unterseen; Dirty Hands, Baar

Decoration
Rufener Events; brogleworks GmbH, Spreitenbach

Catering
Dine & Shine, Urdorf; René Schudel; Nadia Damaso, Zurich

Realisation
brogleworks GmbH

Photos
Christoph Eugster, Bern

RELEVANTE INHALTE UND RENOMMIERTE REDNER STÄRKEN DAS IMAGE DER MARKE FRANKE.

Content Marketing wirkt nicht nur im Internet, sondern auch bei Events; sowohl um mehr Gäste zu einer Veranstaltung zu locken als auch um Aufmerksamkeit in den Online- und Offline-Medien zu generieren. Tatsächliche und informative Inhalte anstatt eigenwerblicher Produktpräsentationen erfreuen sich daher auch in der Live-Kommunikation immer größerer Beliebtheit. Das Ergebnis sind Formate wie Konferenzen, Festivals und Summits – wie auch der Innovation Summit „Think Next by Franke", den die Züricher Agentur Rufener Events sowohl konzipierte als auch umsetzte. Ziel der Veranstaltung war es zu zeigen, dass es nicht nur um vollfunktionale Küchensysteme oder elegante Armaturen geht, sondern darum, die Branchenzukunft weiterzudenken. Herzstück des Events war das Programm: Keynotes von renommierten Rednern und Trendlabs mit Opinionleadern sollten nicht nur die mediale Aufmerksamkeit sicherstellen, sondern auch die Markenidentität und Kundenbindung stärken.

Content marketing works not only on the Internet, but also at events. Both to entice more visitors to an event and to generate interest in online and offline media. Factual and informative content, instead of self-promoting product presentations, is therefore also enjoying increasing popularity in live communication. This results in formats including conferences, festivals and summits – such as the Innovation Summit "Think Next by Franke", which the Zurich agency Rufener Events both designed and realised. The aim of the event was to show that it is not only about fully functional kitchen systems or elegant fittings, but about thinking ahead into the future of the sector. The centrepiece of the event was the programme, with keynotes by renowned speakers and trend labs with opinion leaders, in order to secure the attention of the media, as well as to strengthen the brand identity and customer loyalty.

RELEVANT CONTENT AND RENOWNED SPEAKERS STRENGTHEN THE IMAGE OF THE FRANKE BRAND.

Vorträge und Workshops gaben Einblicke in Themen wie Küchenwelten, Produktdesign, Konsumentenverhalten, Architektur, Wellness und Technologie. Die Inhalte der Veranstaltung wurden von einem Food-Festival mit kulinarischen Experimenten und Networking begleitet. Für eine visuelle Verknüpfung zwischen Inhalten und Marke sorgten Signaletik und Eventdesign, die auf die Corporate Identity und das Corporate Design der Marke abgestimmt waren. Gleiches galt für begleitende Kommunikationsmaßnahmen wie einen Blog und verschiedene Social-Media-Präsenzen. Rufener Events gestaltete ein ganzheitliches Eventdesign, dessen eindeutiger Fokus auf relevantem Content lag.

Presentations and workshops provided insights into topics such as kitchen worlds, product design, consumer behaviour, architecture, wellness and technology. The contents of the event were accompanied by a food festival with culinary experiments and networking. A signage system and an event design aligned with the corporate identity and the corporate design of the brand ensured a visual link between the content and the brand. The same applied to the accompanying communication measures, such as a blog and various social media presences. Rufener Events put together an overall event design whose clear focus was on relevant content.

MERCEDES-BENZ ME CONVENTION
LIGANOVA . THE BRANDRETAIL COMPANY, STUTTGART; JANGLED NERVES GMBH, STUTTGART; ATELIER MARKGRAPH GMBH, FRANKFURT A. MAIN

Location
IAA 2017, Messe Frankfurt, Frankfurt a. Main

Client
Daimler AG, Stuttgart

Month / Year
September 2017

Duration
several days

me Convention
LIGANOVA . The BrandRetail Company, Stuttgart

Architecture Brand Appearance
jangled nerves GmbH, Stuttgart

Communication Brand Appearance
Atelier Markgraph GmbH, Frankfurt a. Main

Photos
LIGANOVA . The BrandRetail Company, Stuttgart; Kristof Lemp, Darmstadt; Markus Nass, Berlin; Karin Berneburg, Frankfurt a. Main; Andreas Keller, Altdorf

EIN MESSEAUFTRITT, DER DIE MARKEN-KOMMUNIKATION VON MORGEN DENKT: ALS DIALOG-PLATTFORM MIT EIGENEM FESTIVAL.

Die Grenzen zwischen Branchen und Kategorien verschwimmen zunehmend – zwischen Messe und Event, zwischen Fachbesucher und Konsument, zwischen Markenpräsentation und Festival. Das Resultat sind neue, interdisziplinäre Konzepte der Markenkommunikation. Wie zum Beispiel die „me Convention" im Rahmen der Mercedes-Benz Dialog-Plattform auf der IAA 2017. Mehr als 150 internationale Speaker kamen auf Einladung von Mercedes-Benz und South by Southwest (SXSW®) nach Frankfurt. Drei Tage lang war die mittlere Ebene des dreigeschossigen Mercedes-Benz-Markenauftritts dem neuen Format vorbehalten – einem integrierten Mix aus Konferenz, Festival und Workshop.

The boundaries between sectors and categories are blurring increasingly – between trade exhibition and event, between specialist visitor and consumer, between brand presentation and festival. The result of this are new and interdisciplinary concepts of brand communication, such as the "me Convention" as part of the Mercedes-Benz Dialogue Platform at IAA 2017. More than 150 international speakers came to Frankfurt upon invitation by Mercedes-Benz and South by Southwest (SXSW®). For three days, the middle level of the three-storey Mercedes-Benz brand presentation was dedicated to the new format – an integrated mix of conference, festival and workshop.

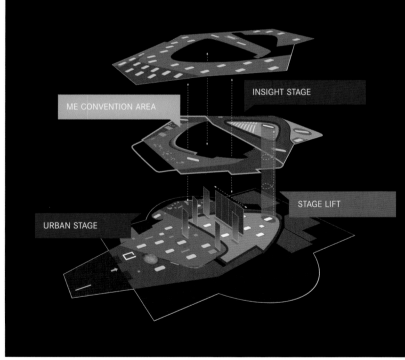

LIGANOVA entwickelte mit der me Convention ein in-
spirierendes Festival- und Konferenz-Format rund um
Themen der Technologie-, Design- und Kreativwirtschaft.
Die Convention war nahtlos in die Dialogplattform von
Mercedes-Benz auf der IAA eingebunden, die von jangled
nerves und Atelier Markgraph konzipiert und umgesetzt
wurde. Inhaltlich fokussierte sich die me Convention auf die
Bereiche New Leadership, New Realities, New Urbanism,
New Creation und New Velocity. In Vorträgen, Panels und
Workshops gaben die mehr als 150 Speaker dazu Einblicke
in ihre Visionen der Zukunft. Ein exklusiver Eingang verband
die me Convention, ihre Co-Working-Spaces, Creator Spots,
Outdoor- und Chill-Out-Areas und den eigenen Foodmarket
mit der Stadt. Konzerte und Networking-Events verlängerten
den Messeauftritt in die Frankfurter Innenstadt und machten
ihn auch über die Messe hinaus zugänglich. Inhalte und
Geschehnisse rund um die me Convention wurden online
aufgegriffen und über die eigenen Social-Media-Kanäle
verbreitet.

With the me Convention, LIGANOVA developed an inspiring festival and conference format surrounding the topics
of technology, design and the creative industry. The convention was incorporated seamlessly into the IAA, which
was conceived and realised by jangled nerves and atelier
markgraph. The content of the me Convention focussed on
the areas of New Leadership, New Realities, New Urbanism,
New Creation and New Velocity. More than 150 speakers
provided insights into their visions of the future through
presentations, panels and workshops. An exclusive entrance
linked the town with the me Convention, its co-working
spaces, creator sports, outdoor and chill-out areas and its own
food market. Concerts and networking events extended the
trade fair presence into the city centre of Frankfurt and made
it accessible beyond the exhibition grounds. The contents
and events surrounding the me Convention were taken up
online, as well as spread through their social media channels.

AN EXHIBITION PRESENCE THAT CON-SIDERS THE BRAND COMMUNICATION OF TOMORROW: AS DIALOGUE PLATFORM WITH ITS OWN FESTIVAL.

THE PARISIAN MACAO
GRAND OPENING
UNIPLAN GMBH & CO. KG, HONG KONG

Location
The Parisian Macao, Macao

Client
Sands China Ltd., Macao

Month / Year
September 2016

Duration
1 day

Architecture / Design / Graphics / Lighting / Music / Artists / Show acts
Uniplan GmbH & Co. KG, Hong Kong

Photos
8ightPro Studio, Hong Kong

DIE ERÖFFNUNG EINES LUXUS-HOTELS WIRD ZU EINEM FULMINANTEN PARISER SZENENBILD.

Das 2016 neu eröffnete Luxus-Hotel „The Parisian Macao" möchte sich mit seinem romantischen, stilvollen und eleganten Ambiente hervorheben. Ein Hauch von Paris soll die Gäste umgeben. Naheliegend, dass Uniplan Hong Kong für die Eröffnung im September 2016 Paris nach Macao holte. Die Gäste erwartete mit Betreten des Hauses eine fantastische Welt mit Pariser Sehenswürdigkeiten, Geräuschen, Gerüchen und Geschmäckern. Die zentrale Botschaft „Werde ein Teil von Paris" sollte in jedem Element der Veranstaltung spürbar werden.

The luxury hotel "The Parisian Macao" reopened in 2016 seeks to distinguish itself through its romantic, stylish and elegant ambience, with a Parisian flair surrounding the guests. It follows therefore that Uniplan Hong Kong brought Paris to Macao for the opening in September 2016. Upon entering the building, a fantastical world of Parisian sights, smells and tastes awaited the guests. The central message "Become a part of Paris" was designed to be evident in each element of the event.

THE OPENING OF A LUXURY HOTEL BECOMES A FULMINANT PARISIAN SCENOGRAPHY.

Pantomimen, Karikaturisten, Pétanque-Spieler, Zauberer und Straßenhändler interagierten mit den Gästen und inszenierten einen Spaziergang durch die Pariser Straßen. Animationen sowie Orchester- und Tanzperformances sorgten für eine fulminante Nacht. Der nachgebaute und im Vergleich zum Original fast halb so hohe Eiffelturm des Hotels wurde zu einer der weltgrößten Bühnen. Eine maßgeschneiderte 30-minütige Show beeindruckte mit bildgewaltigen Filmen und erstaunlichen Bühnensets. Das Highlight war ein eigens gebauter, acht Meter hoher Heißluftballon, der die Hauptdarsteller auf die Bühne brachte. Den Abschluss der Aufführung bildete ein multimediales Finale mit Gesang, Feuerwerk und einer Lichtinszenierung auf dem Eiffelturm.

Pantomimes, caricaturists, pétanque players, magicians and street vendors interacted with the guests and simulated a walk through the streets of Paris. Animations, as well as orchestra and dance performances, ensured a fulminant night. The imitation Eiffel Tower at the hotel, almost half as high as the original, became one of the world's biggest stages. A customised 30-minute show impressed the viewers with visually stunning films and extraordinary stage sets. The highlight was a specially built, eight-metre-high hot-air balloon that brought the main actors to the stage. The performance was crowned by a multimedia finale with singing, fireworks and a light show on the Eiffel Tower.

OLYMPUS PERSPECTIVE PLAYGROUND
VITAMIN E – GESELLSCHAFT FÜR KOMMUNIKATION MBH, HAMBURG

Location
Kraftwerk Berlin, Berlin

Client
Olympus Europa SE & Co. KG, Hamburg

Month / Year
September 2017

Duration
several weeks

Artists / Show acts
Patrick Shearn / Poetic Kinetics, Los Angeles; Liz West, Manchester; Thilo Frank, Berlin; Adam Scales + Ari + Pierre Berthelomeau, Rotterdam; Quintessenz, Hanover / Berlin; Gabriel Pulecio, New York; Xaver Hirsch, Berlin; flora&faunavisions, Berlin

Others
Leigh Sachwitz, Berlin (Curator); Andreas H. Bitesnich, Vienna (Photo exhibition); Olympus Visionaries (Photo exhibition)

Photos
Klaus Bossemeyer, Münster; VITAMIN E – Gesellschaft für Kommunikation mbH, Hamburg

EIN KÜNSTLERISCHER SPIELPLATZ FÜR FOTOGRAFIE LÄDT BESUCHER ZUM WOMÖGLICH KREATIVSTEN PRODUKTTEST EIN.

The event concept launched in 2013 under the name "Olympus Photography Playground" is now among the most well-known successful projects in live communication. Together with VITAMIN E, Olympus realised the idea of a photographic art trail, which has since been shown 17 times in various adaptations in Germany, as well as France, the Netherlands, Austria, Switzerland, Spain and Denmark. Equipped with borrowed Olympus cameras, visitors can explore the interactive exhibition designed by varying artists, capture it in photographs and unleash their own creativity. This exceptional concept was able to attract over 350,000 visitors and gain more than ten national and international awards.

Das unter dem Namen „Olympus Photography Playground" im Jahr 2013 gestartete Eventkonzept gehört heute zu den bekanntesten Erfolgsprojekten in der Live-Kommunikation. Zusammen mit VITAMIN E realisierte Olympus die Idee eines Fotokunstpfades, der mittlerweile 17 Mal in Deutschland sowie in Frankreich, den Niederlanden, Österreich, der Schweiz, Spanien und Dänemark in verschiedenen Adaptionen umgesetzt wurde. Ausgestattet mit geliehenen Olympus-Kameras können Besucher die von wechselnden Künstlern gestaltete interaktive Ausstellung erkunden, fotografisch festhalten und selbst kreativ werden. Mehr als 350.000 Besucher und über zehn nationale sowie internationale Auszeichnungen hat dieses außergewöhnliche Konzept für sich gewinnen können.

AN ARTISTIC PLAY-GROUND FOR PHOTO-GRAPHY INVITES VISITORS TO PERHAPS THE MOST CREATIVE PRODUCT TEST.

Unter dem heutigen Namen „Olympus Perspective Playground" besteht das Event nicht mehr alleinig aus einem künstlerischen, erlebnisorientierten Spielplatz für Fotografie. Die Geschäftsbereiche „Medical Systems" und „Scientific Solutions" wurden integriert und ergänzen das Erlebnis mit einer Kombination aus Kunst und Wissenschaft. Im September 2017 kehrte der Perspective Playground wieder an den Ort zurück, an dem alles begann: nach Berlin. Zum 17. Mal wurden die Besucher eingeladen, die interaktiven Arbeiten verschiedener Künstler und Kollektive fotografisch zu erkunden – beim letzten Event unter anderem von Poetic Kinetics, Liz West, Thilo Frank und Adam Scales + Ari + Pierre Berthelomeau.

Under the current name "Olympus Perspective Playground", the event no longer consists solely of an artistic, experience-orientated playground for photography. The business divisions of "Medical Systems" and "Scientific Solutions" have been integrated and extend the experience with a combination of art and science. In September 2017, the Perspective Playground returned to the place where it all began: Berlin. Visitors were invited for the 17th time to explore the interactive work of various artists and collections photographically – at the latest event these included Poetic Kinetics, Liz West, Thilo Frank and Adam Scales + Ari + Pierre Berthelomeau.

Jede Zielgruppe hat unterschiedliche Bedürfnisse und Erwartungen. Dementsprechend sind Eventkonzepte im Idealfall nicht nur auf den Absender, sondern vor allem auf die Empfänger zugeschnitten.

PARTNERS: VERBUNDENE UNTERNEHMEN, (ZWISCHEN-) HÄNDLER ODER VERTRIEBS- PARTNER, DEREN INFORMA- TIONSHINTERGRUND BEREITS AUF EINE EBENE GEBRACHT WURDE ODER NUN GEBRACHT WERDEN SOLL. DEMENT- SPRECHEND HOMOGEN IST DIESE ZIELGRUPPE ZUSAMMEN- GESTELLT, DEREN ANSPRACHE DIREKT UND EXTREM ZIEL- ORIENTIERT GEHANDHABT WERDEN KANN.

Each target group has different requirements and expectations. Event concepts are therefore ideally not only geared towards the addressor, but especially towards the recipients.

PARTNERS: THESE ARE ASSOCIATED COMPANIES, (INTERMEDIARY) DISTRIBUTORS OR SALES PARTNERS WHO ALREADY HAVE A CERTAIN LEVEL OF BACKGROUND INFORMATION, OR FOR WHOM THIS IS NOW TO BE PROVIDED. THIS TARGET GROUP THEREFORE HAS A HOMOGENEOUS COMPOSITION AND CAN BE APPEALED TO DIRECTLY AND IN A VERY TARGET-ORIENTATED MANNER.

VOLKSWAGEN INTERNATIONAL PARTNER MEETING
BLACKSPACE GMBH, MUNICH

Location
Tempodrom, Berlin; Kraftwerk, Berlin

Client
Volkswagen AG, Wolfsburg

Month / Year
June 2017

Duration
several days

Concept / Design / Execution / Coordination
BLACKSPACE GmbH, Munich

Architecture
Vierwerken, Munich

Lighting
Four to one Lighting Design GmbH, Bornheim

Media
TFN GmbH & Co. KG, Hamburg

Direction
Music Company Media Productions OHG, Munich

Music
Nitro Booking GmbH, Reichertshausen

Catering
VW Catering, Wolfsburg

Realisation
a&a expo international b.v., Wijk bij Duurstede

Photos
Stefan Bösl / KBUMM.Agentur, Ingolstadt

Mehr als 4.000 Händler und Importeure aus aller Welt waren zum „Volkswagen International Partner Meeting 2017" eingeladen. Unter dem Motto „We make the future real. Together." sollte nicht nur ein Blick in die Zukunft gewährt, sondern auch Gemeinschaft kommuniziert werden. Mit diesen Zielen entwickelte BLACKSPACE ein neues Format, das die internationalen Besucher in die deutsche Hauptstadt führte. Im Berliner Tempodrom präsentierte Volkswagen über drei Tage hinweg die Neuausrichtung der Marke. Eine Keynote, fahraktive Präsentationen, Filmbespielungen und eine Augmented-Reality-Show thematisierten aktuelle Herausforderungen und mögliche Lösungen zu den Fragen: Wie definiert sich der Begriff „Mobilität" neu? Wie sehen die zukünftigen Fahrzeug- und Antriebskonzepte aus? Wo und wie kaufe ich in Zukunft mein Auto? Die Einbindung des Publikums und eine Lichtshow mit 64 Light Beams spiegelten das Motto „Together" inhaltlich wie auch räumlich.

EINE KULINARISCHE, KULTURELLE UND RÄUMLICHE FUSION SPIEGELT DIE MISCHUNG DER GÄSTE WIDER UND SYMBOLISIERT DIE GEMEINSCHAFT.

A CULINARY, CULTURAL AND SPATIAL FUSION REFLECTS THE MIX OF GUESTS AND SYMBOLISES COMMUNITY.

More than 4,000 dealerships and importers from around the world were invited to the "Volkswagen International Partner Meeting 2017." In accordance with the motto "We make the future real. Together", it was designed not only to look towards the future, but also to communicate a sense of community. With these aims in mind, BLACKSPACE developed a new format that brought international visitors to the German capital. Volkswagen presented the new brand orientation over the course of three days at the Berlin Tempodrom. A keynote, active driving presentations, film animations and an augmented reality show cast a spotlight on current challenges and possible solutions to the questions: how is the notion of "mobility" being redefined? What do the vehicle and engine concepts of the future look like? Where and how will I buy my car in the future? The involvement of the visitors and a lighting show with 64 light beams reflected the motto "Together" both spatially and in terms of content.

Das abendliche Dinner-Event ging mit einem Location-wechsel in das imposante Berliner Kraftwerk einher. Ein kulinarischer Mix aus asiatischem Sushi, amerikanischen Burgern, russischem Pelmeni und der Berliner Currywurst griff die Internationalität der Gäste auf. Im Eventdesign fand sich eine Mischung aus Urban Gardening und Street-Food-Elementen wieder. Zwischen Erdbeerbeet und Tomaten-strauch entfaltete sich eine Markthalle mit unterschiedlichen Food-Courts und für drei Nächte die längste Bar Berlins. Ein Highlight hinter der Theke waren die außergewöhnlichen Barkeeper: Roboter sorgten für die Getränkeproduktion und knüpften an das zukunftsorientierte Motto an.

The evening dinner event saw a change of location to the impressive Berlin power plant. A culinary mix of Asian sushi, American burgers, Russian pelmeni and Berlin curry sausage reflected the internationality of the guests. The event design included a mix of urban gardening and street food elements. A market hall stretched between the strawberry bed and a tomato vine, with various food courts and what was for three nights the longest bar in Berlin. The unusual bar keepers were a highlight behind the bar counter: Robots provided the drinks and embodied the future-orientated motto.

AUDI DEALER MEETING CÔTE D'AZUR

SCHMIDHUBER, MUNICH; MUTABOR, HAMBURG

Location
Aéroport Cannes Mandelieu, Cannes; Gare Maritime, Cannes; Château Sainte Roseline, Les Arcs; Club Dauphin, Saint-Jean Cap-Ferrat

Client
AUDI AG, Ingolstadt

Month / Year
November 2017

Duration
several days

Dramaturgy / Direction / Coordination / Architecture / Design / Graphics / Decoration
SCHMIDHUBER Brand Experience GmbH, Munich; MUTABOR Brand Experience, Hamburg

Lighting
FOUR TO ONE LIGHTING DESIGN GMBH, Bornheim; PRG AG, Hamburg

Media
TFN GmbH & Co. KG, Hamburg; CT Germany, Dettingen / Teck

Films
MUTABOR Brand Experience; Betty Mü, Anzing

Music
DJ Sepalot, Munich

Catering
Feinkost Käfer, Munich; Château Sainte Roseline, Les Arcs

Realisation
metron Vilshofen GmbH, Vilshofen

Others
AVE Audio Visual Equipment Verhengsten GmbH & Co., Bergisch Gladbach (Audio)

Photos
Tobias Sagmeister Photography, Bad Gögging

Für das Audi Dealer Meeting 2017 lud der Autobauer Händler und Importeure aus der ganzen Welt nach Südfrankreich ein. Ein insgesamt dreiwöchiges Event verband fünf Veranstaltungsorte an der Côte d'Azur. Das von Schmidhuber und Mutabor entwickelte Konzept samt Gestaltung ließ die Gäste für jeweils zwei Tage Produkte, Fahrzeuge und Neuheiten von Audi erleben. Nach Ankunft und Akkreditierung am Flughafen in Nizza fuhren die Teilnehmer im neuen Audi A8 durch die traumhafte Landschaft Südfrankreichs zum Lunch in den Club Dauphin. Im Anschluss präsentierte Audi sein exklusives Portfolio der Audi Sport Collection von Kleidung und Accessoires zwischen Holzfässern und Weinflaschen auf dem Weingut Château Sainte Roseline.

AUDI FAHRZEUGE, PRODUKTE UND NEUHEITEN – INSZENIERT IM RAHMEN EINER JEWEILS ZWEITÄGIGEN, KONTRASTREICHEN REISE.

For the Audi Dealer Meeting 2017, the car manufacturer invited dealerships and importers from around the world to the south of France. An event spanning three weeks in total linked five event venues on the Côte d'Azur. The concept and design put together by Schmidhuber and Mutabor allowed guests to experience Audi products, vehicles and novelties for two days at a time. After arrival and accreditation at the airport in Nice, the participants drove in a new Audi A8 through the fabulous landscape of southern France to Club Dauphin for lunch. Following on from this, Audi presented its exclusive portfolio of clothes and accessories from the Audi Sports Collection, between wooden barrels and wine bottles on the Château Sainte Roseline vineyard.

AUDI VEHICLES, PRODUCTS AND NOVELTIES – PRESENTED AS PART OF A TWO-DAY JOURNEY RICH IN CONTRAST.

Die Abendveranstaltung im Gare Maritime in Cannes inszenierte den „automobilen Traum". Eine zweieinhalbstündige
Live-Show mit Tänzern, Musikern und Sängern performte
die „Gegenwart als Auftakt der Zukunft". Höhepunkt des
Händlermeetings war die Produktshow im Hangar 16 am
Flughafen Mandelieu. Um die Artificial-Intelligence-Techno-
logie von Audi zu demonstrieren, wurde der gesamte Hangar zu einem Serverraum. Live-Performances und kinetische
Bühnenelemente visualisierten die Lernfähigkeit der intelligenten Modellgeneration und setzten die präsentierten
Fahrzeuge in Szene. Die Serverstruktur setzte sich in einer
ergänzenden Ausstellung mit Zukunftsthemen und Visionen
von Digitalisierung, Technik und Design fort.

The evening event at the Gare Maritime in Cannes set the
scene for the "automobile dream". A two-and-a-half-hour
live show with dancers, musicians and singers performed
the "present as a prelude to the future". The highlight of the
dealer meeting was the product show in hangar 16 at Mandelieu airport. To demonstrate the Audi artificial intelligence
technology, the whole hangar was turned into a server room.
Live performances and kinetic stage elements visualised the
learning capability of the intelligent model generation and
provided a stage for the presented vehicles. The server
structure continued in a complementary exhibition on the
subject of the future and visions of digitisation, technology
and design.

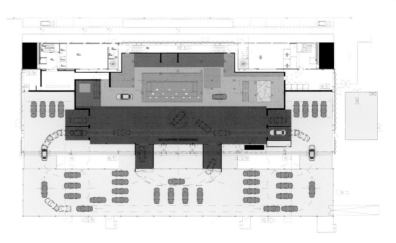

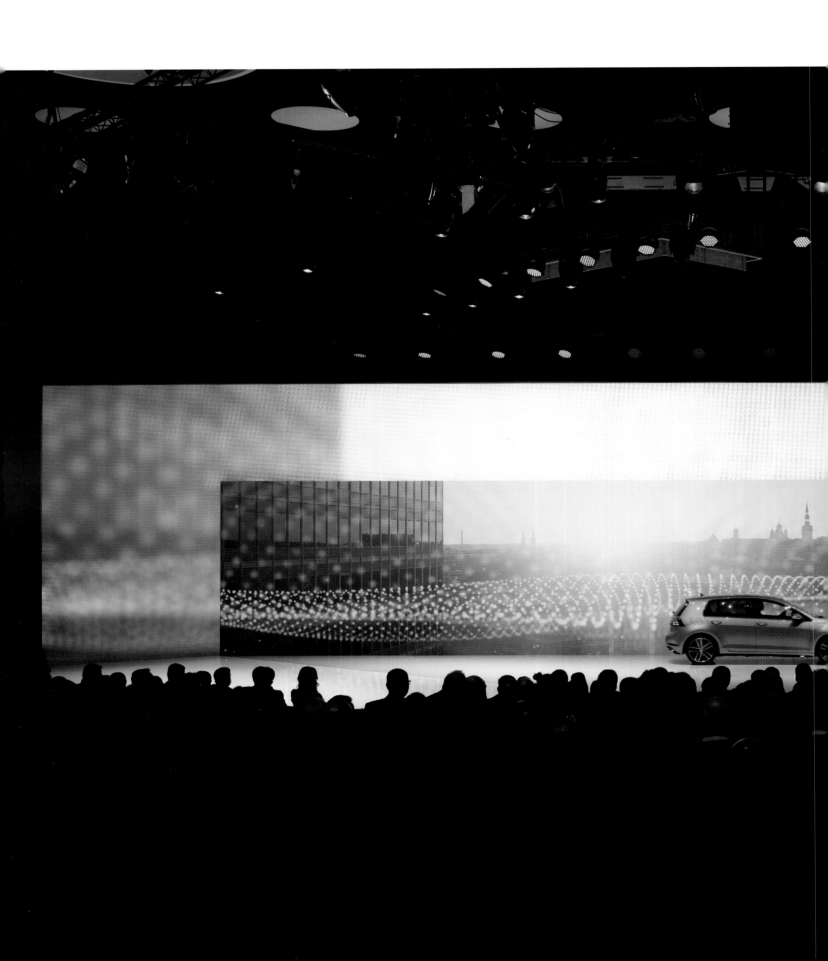

VOLKSWAGEN
DEALER CONVENTION
STAGG & FRIENDS GMBH, DUSSELDORF

Location
World Conference Center Bonn, Bonn

Client
Volkswagen AG, Wolfsburg

Month / Year
January 2017

Duration
several days

Dramaturgy / Architecture / Design / Graphics
STAGG & FRIENDS GmbH, Dusseldorf

Direction / Coordination
STAGG & FRIENDS GmbH; QUINTONS CONCEPT show productions, Dusseldorf

Lighting
PRG XL Video, Dusseldorf

Artists / Show acts
hillentertainment, Leverkusen

Decoration
Late Night Concepts Veranstaltungsproduktion GmbH & Co. KG, Werne

Catering
Broich Premium Catering GmbH, Meerbusch

Realisation
Concret GmbH, Cologne

Photos
Daniel Hübler / Bild im Kasten, Neuss

Über 1.000 Handelspartner der Marke Volkswagen wurden im Januar 2017 in das World Conference Center in Bonn geladen. Die Jahresauftaktveranstaltung diente sowohl dazu, die Partner über die strategische Ausrichtung auf dem Laufenden zu halten als auch den angestrebten Zukunftswandel zu kommunizieren. STAGG & FRIENDS entwickelte das inszenatorische Gesamtkonzept, das die verschiedenen Ziele und Themen in einem zukunftsgerichteten Business-Meeting zusammenführte.

SZENISCH-REALE RÄUME ERZÄHLEN VON ZUKÜNFTIGEN MARKEN-TOUCH-POINTS UND DEM KUNDENERLEBNIS IM DIGITALEN ZEITALTER.

SCENIC-REAL SPACES TELL OF FUTURE BRAND TOUCH-POINTS AND THE CUS-TOMER EXPERIENCE IN THE DIGITAL AGE.

Over 1,000 trade partners of the Volkswagen brand were invited in January 2017 to the World Conference Center in Bonn. The event to mark the start of the year served both to keep partners informed about the strategic direction, as well as to communicate the striven for future change. STAGG & FRIENDS developed the setting and overall concept, which brought together the various goals and themes within a future-orientated business meeting.

Im Sinne eines zeitgemäßen und zielgruppenorientierten Handelsmarketings lud die Veranstaltung dazu ein, sich in das Innere der Marke zu begeben und das Kundenerlebnis im digitalen Zeitalter zu erleben. Charakteristische Touchpoints skizzierten zukünftige Berührungspunkte zwischen Kunde und Marke. Die digitale Händlerplattform wurde mithilfe eines szenisch-realen Umfelds entlang der Customer Journey vorgestellt, was die Präsentation durch das Management räumlich unterstützte. Die begleitende Medienarchitektur sorgte für große Bilder und durch die überraschende Erweiterung des bespielbaren LED-Portals für einen visuell scheinbar endlosen Horizont. Highlight der Veranstaltung war die Inszenierung des neuen Volkswagen I.D. – ein Auto, das 2020 in Serie geht und eine Ikone für die Zukunft der Marke symbolisiert. Ähnlich zukunftsgerichtet waren zwei Pop-up-Stores, in denen die Händler den Virtual-Reality-Auftritt der Marke und den Veranstaltungsclaim „Unterwegs in die Zukunft" erleben konnten.

In accordance with contemporary and target-group-orienta-ted trade marketing, the event invited the guests to engage with the core of the brand and with the customer experience in the digital age. Characteristic touchpoints sketched future points of contact between the customer and the brand. The digital trade platform was presented with the help of a scenic-real environment along the customer journey that provided spatial support for the presentation by the management. The accompanying media architecture offered large images and a visually seemingly endless horizon, due to the surprising extension of the LED portal that could be animated. The highlight of the event was the staging of the new Volkswagen I.D. – a car that will go into serial production in 2020 and symbolises an icon for the future of the brand. Two pop-up stores, where trade partners could experience a virtual reality presentation of the brand and the event claim "On the road to the future", were similarly future-orientated.

Jede Zielgruppe hat unterschiedliche Bedürfnisse und Erwartungen. Dementsprechend sind Eventkonzepte im Idealfall nicht nur auf den Absender, sondern vor allem auf die Empfänger zugeschnitten.

FRIENDS: EIN EXKLUSIVER UND VOR ALLEM AUSGEWÄHLTER KREIS AN GÄSTEN, DER SICH AUS DEN UNTERSCHIEDLICHSTEN ZIELGRUPPEN ZUSAMMENSETZT: PARTNER, KUNDEN, FANS, WEGBEGLEITER, (LOKAL-)PROMINENZ, (BRANCHEN- UND UNTERNEHMENS-)VIPS, EHREN-GÄSTE UND MEDIENVERTRETER. TROTZ KULTURELLER UND GESELLSCHAFTLICHER HETERO-GENITÄT EINT SIE DIE TATSACHE, DASS SIE DEM GASTGEBER FREUNDSCHAFTLICH GESONNEN UND MEIST EINER DIREKTEN EINLADUNG GEFOLGT SIND.

Each target group has different requirements and expectations. Event concepts are therefore ideally not only geared towards the addressor, but especially towards the recipients.

FRIENDS: FRIENDS ARE AN EXCLUSIVE AND SELECTED CIRCLE OF GUESTS COMPOSED OF A WIDE RANGE OF TARGET GROUPS: PARTNERS, CUSTOMERS, FANS, COMPANIONS, (LOCAL) CELEBRITIES, VIPS (FROM COMPANIES AND THE SECTOR), GUESTS OF HONOUR AND MEDIA REPRESENTATIVES. DESPITE CULTURAL AND SOCIAL HETEROGENEITY, THEY ARE UNITED BY THE FACT THAT THEY ARE ON FRIENDLY TERMS WITH THE HOST AND MOSTLY RESPONDED TO A DIRECT INVITATION.

MARC CAIN FASHION SHOW FALL/WINTER 2017
MARC CAIN GMBH

Location
Ehemaliges Kaiserliches Telegraphenamt, Berlin

Client
Marc Cain GmbH, Bodelshausen

Month / Year
January 2017

Duration
1 day

Architecture / Design / Lighting
Nowadays GmbH, Berlin

Graphics
Marc Cain GmbH

Music
John Gürtler, Berlin (DJ); Oriel Quartett, Berlin

Artists / Show acts
Iconic Talentmanagement UG & Co. KG, Hamburg; Spin Model Management GmbH, Hamburg; Modelwerk Modelagentur GmbH, Hamburg; M4 Models Management GmbH, Hamburg; Seeds Management GmbH, Berlin

Decoration
Marc Cain GmbH; Nowadays GmbH

Photos
Marc Cain GmbH

GLAMOURÖSE STREET-STYLE-LOOKS KLASSISCH-MODERN INSZENIERT – MIT GRAZILEN BALLERINEN IN SCHWARZ-WEISS, STREICHQUARTETT UND DJ-BEATS.

Festliche Outfits brauchen ein ebenso festliches Ambiente. Darum wählte Marc Cain das prachtvolle ehemalige Telegraphenamt für die Fashion Show Berlin Herbst/Winter 2017. Das von außen eindrucksvolle Gebäude vermag auch im Inneren mit einem prunkvollen Raum, mehreren Galerien und verspiegelten Decken zu beeindrucken. Entsprechend glanzvoll und glamourös zeigten sich sowohl die Outfits wie die Gäste. Zugeschnitten auf die Mode, Architektur und Atmosphäre stand die Fashion Show unter dem Motto „Ballet Magnifique".

Festive outfits require an equally festive ambience. For this reason, Marc Cain chose the grandiose former telegraph office for the Fashion Show Berlin Fall/Winter 2017. The build ding that is already impressive from the outside is equally formidable in the interior, with an ostentatious room, several galleries and mirrored ceilings. The outfits and guests presented themselves as suitably glittering and glamourous. Tailored towards fashion, architecture and atmosphere, the fashion show was under the motto "Ballet Magnifique".

GLAMOROUS STREET STYLE LOOKS WITH A CLASSICAL-MODERN STAGING – WITH SVELTE BALLERINAS IN BLACK-WHITE, A STRING QUARTET AND DJ BEATS.

Der Showroom, der erst wenige Minuten vor dem Beginn geöffnet wurde, präsentierte sich in schwarzem, elegantem Eventdesign. Die einzelnen Bereiche des M-förmigen Glitzer-Laufstegs wurden durch dunkel glänzende, transparente Gazevorhänge getrennt. Darüber schwebte ein Himmel aus schwarzen Tüllröcken und rosafarbenen Ballettschuhen. Das bekannte und markante Model Kris Gottschalk eröffnete die Show mit einem Statement-Shirt, auf dem „Don't walk – dance" stand. Ihr folgten grazile Ballerinen in langen, fließenden Röcken und beschrifteten Shirts – „Yes, we dance". Begleitet wurde die Eröffnung sowie die gesamte Show von einem Mix aus klassischer Musik und modernen Beats, gespielt von einem Streichquartett und einem DJ.

The showroom, which was opened just a few minutes before the start, presented itself as a black and elegant event design. The individual areas of the M-shaped glitzy runway were separated by shiny dark and transparent gauze curtains. Above it floated a sky of black tulle skirts and pink ballet shoes. The well-known and striking model Kris Gottschalk opened the show with a statement shirt with "Don't walk – dance" written on it. She was followed by graceful ballerinas in long flowing skirts and imprinted shirts – "Yes, we dance". The opening and the whole show were accompanied by a mix of classical music and modern beats – played by a string quartet and a DJ.

JAHRESBESTENEHRUNG DER IHK KARLSRUHE

PXNG.LI GMBH, KARLSRUHE

Location
Gartenhalle der KMK, Karlsruhe

Client
IHK Karlsruhe, Karlsruhe

Month / Year
November 2016

Duration
1 day

Dramaturgy / Direction / Coordination / Architecture / Design / Graphics / Media / Films
PXNG.LI GmbH, Karlsruhe

Lighting
hell begeistert. GmbH, Ötigheim

Artists / Show acts
Pierre M. Krause, Karlsruhe; Les Brünettes, Hamburg

Decoration
Audiovisual Veranstaltungstechnik Pascal Fitterer, Durmersheim; Messe- und Eventtechnik Mitja Gleich, Karlsruhe

Realisation
Audiovisual Veranstaltungstechnik Pascal Fitterer

Photos
PXNG.LI GmbH, Karlsruhe

Die besten Absolventen und Absolventinnen der IHK Karlsruhe werden alljährlich in der Karlsruher Gartenhalle geehrt. Eine große Festveranstaltung dient der Jahresbestenehrung als Rahmen, bei der über 190 Preisträger auf unterhaltsame Weise erwähnt werden sollen. Wichtig ist den Gastgebern, dass auch der letzte Preisträger die gebührende Spannung und Aufmerksamkeit erhält.

The best graduates at IHK Karlsruhe are honoured every year at the Gartenhalle in Karlsruhe. A major celebratory event serves as a framework for the best-of-the-year awards, at which over 190 prize winners are mentioned in an entertaining manner. It is important to the hosts that even the last award winner is given the due attention and interest.

EINE EHRUNGS-VERANSTALTUNG ALS 80ER-JAHRE TV-QUIZSHOW – MIT TELETEXTANZEIGEN FÜR DIE PREISTRÄGER.

Das Bühnen- und Ehrungskonzept 2016 stammt von PXNG.LI und reiste mit den Gästen zurück in die 80er-Jahre. Die Bühnengestaltung samt Konzept orientierte sich an einer TV-Quizshow. Drei Leinwände wurden mithilfe von Holzrahmen und erhabenen Designelementen zu über-dimensionalen Retro-Fernsehern. Dabei wurden auch kleine Details wie eine leichte Krümmung der damaligen Bild-schirme bedacht und in der Rückprojektion eingebaut. Der Look der Screens war an verschiedene TV-Shows angelehnt. Schriftzüge im Stil von Teletextanzeigen und Quizantworten präsentierten die Preisträger und sollten die Spannung bei jeder Namensnennung aufrechterhalten. In Manier eines Late-Night-Show-Moderators führte Pierre M. Krause durch das Programm und wurde von der Acapella-Gruppe „Les Brünettes" musikalisch unterstützt.

The stage and awards concept stemmed from PXNG.LI in 2016 and travelled with the guests back into the 1980s. The stage design and the concept were orientated towards a TV quiz show. Three screens were turned into large-scale retro TVs with the help of wooden frames and grand design elements. Even minor details, such as the slight curvature of the screens at the time, were taken into consideration and incorporated into the retrojection. The look of the screens evoked various TV shows. Lettering in the style of teletext messages and quiz answers presented the prize winners and was designed to maintain the same level of interest in every name mentioned. In the manner of a late-night show presenter, Pierre M. Krause provided guidance through the programme and was accompanied musically by the a capella group "Les Brünettes".

AN AWARDS EVENT AS A 1980S TV QUIZ SHOW – WITH TELETEXT MESSAGES FOR THE PRIZE WINNERS.

150 JAHRE TENGELMANN. WEITERHANDELN.
MATT CIRCUS GMBH, COLOGNE

Location
Tengelmann TECHNIKUM, Mülheim a. d. Ruhr

Client
Tengelmann Warenhandelsgesellschaft KG, Mülheim a. d. Ruhr

Month / Year
September 2017

Duration
1 day

Media
Choreograffiti Limited, Cologne; PI spirit Production International GmbH, Cologne

Artists / Show acts
querspringer, Cologne

Decoration
BALLONI GmbH, Cologne

Catering
Broich Premium Catering GmbH, Meerbusch

Realisation
DEKO-Service Lenzen GmbH, Lohmar

Others
nvl² Nossbach Veranstaltungslogistik GmbH, Cologne (Event technology); Guest-One GmbH, Wuppertal (Participator management); Detlef Altenbeck, Bonn (conceptual support); Rolf Maier GmbH & Co. KG, Bestwig (Regie); ASP Eventrealisation GmbH, Essen (Technology); JKR-Events, Dortmund (Technology); Neumann&Müller GmbH & Co. KG, Cologne (Technology)

Photos
Tengelmann Warenhandelsgesellschaft KG, Mülheim a. d. Ruhr

Jubiläumsveranstaltungen laufen zumeist nach ähnlichem Schema ab, selten wird etwas Neues ausprobiert. Die Unternehmensgruppe Tengelmann hat es zusammen mit MATT CIRCUS gewagt und inszenierte ihren 150. Geburtstag als persönliche, unkonventionelle Familienfeier. Treffpunkt für die rund 400 meist prominenten Gäste war das TECHNIKUM, die hauseigene Location am Stammsitz in Mülheim. Das traditionelle Familienunternehmen sollte authentisch und offen als vertraute Gemeinschaft präsentiert werden. Im konzeptionellen Fokus standen Inhalte statt Show- oder Media-Content.

Anniversary events usually follow a similar pattern and it is rare to try something new, but the Tengelmann corporate group, together with MATT CIRCUS, ventured to do so and staged its 150th anniversary as a personal, unconventional family celebration. The gathering place for around 400 mostly high-profile guests was the TECHNIKUM on their own site at the head office in Mülheim. The traditional family enterprise sought to be presented as authentic and open, as a close-knit community. The conceptual focus was on content, instead of on show or media content.

EIN FIRMENJUBILÄUM WIRD ALS FAMILIEN-FEIER INSZENIERT. IM WOHNZIMMER WIRD GEPLAUDERT, IN DER KÜCHE GEMEINSAM GEKOCHT.

So wurde die Bühne zum „Wohnzimmer", in dem sich die Inhaberfamilie, Tochterunternehmen und Mitarbeiter entspannt über die Vergangenheit und Zukunft unterhielten. Zusammen mit einem TV-Koch wurde in der illustrierten Küche live der nächste Gang zubereitet und dabei über Persönliches geplaudert. Politiker und Wirtschaftsvertreter standen für ihre Rednerbeiträge „spontan" nach einem Glasklingeln auf und sprachen am Tisch. Das Ziel, eine authentische, offene und familiäre Atmosphäre zu erzeugen, wurde in allen Programmpunkten und Inhalten bedacht. Um die „Storys" der Veranstaltung herauszuarbeiten, wurden im Vorfeld mit allen Bühnenprotagonisten Interviews gefuhrt und lediglich grobe Gesprächsleitfäden erstellt. Die Antworten der Gesprächsrunden im „Wohnzimmer" und der „Küche" waren nicht vorgegeben, der Ablauf war bewusst weitestgehend ungeprobt und daher spontan.

A COMPANY ANNIVERSARY IS STAGED AS A FAMILY CELEBRATION, CHATTING IN THE LIVING ROOM AND COOKING TOGETHER IN THE KITCHEN.

The stage was therefore a "living room" in which the owner family, subsidiaries and employees conversed casually about the past and the future. The next course was prepared live in the illustrated kitchen, together with a TV chef, whilst chatting about personal matters. Politicians and economists stood up "spontaneously" after tapping on a glass to contribute their speeches, speaking at the table. The aim of generating an authentic, open and casual atmosphere was considered in all aspects of the programme and contents. In order to work out the "stories" of the event, interviews were carried out in advance with all stage protagonists, setting out just rough conversational threads. The answers given during the discussion rounds in the "living room" and in the "kitchen" were not prescribed. The procedure was deliberately largely unrehearsed and therefore spontaneous.

MUSTANG STREET ART LAB
DREINULL AGENTUR FÜR MEDIATAINMENT GMBH & CO. KG, BERLIN; UNIT-BERLIN GMBH, BERLIN; UNDPLUS, BERLIN

Location
SevenStar Gallery, Berlin

Client
MUSTANG GmbH, Künzelsau

Month / Year
July 2017

Duration
several days

Dramaturgy / Direction / Coordination / Graphics
DREINULL Agentur für Mediatainment GmbH & Co. KG, Berlin

Architecture / Design
unit-berlin GmbH, Berlin

Artists / Show acts
UNDPLUS artist selection: Nomad, Berlin; Jule Waibel, Berlin; SuperBlast, Berlin; Clemens Behr, Berlin

Decoration
BALLONI GmbH Berlin, Berlin; unit-berlin GmbH

Catering
Mogg, Berlin

Others
PAM events Veranstaltungsgesellschaft mbH, Berlin (Technology); BIERBIER, Berlin; WildCorn GmbH, Berlin; Berliner Brandstifter GmbH, Berlin

Photos
Marcus Zumbansen, Berlin

Messen sind interessante Kontaktpunkte zu Zielgruppen, die man sonst selten so komprimiert und gezielt ausgerichtet erreichen kann. Gleichzeitig gehört es sicherlich zu einer der schwierigsten Aufgaben, die Aufmerksamkeit von Messebesuchern zu gewinnen. Die Dichte an Reizen, Angeboten und Gesprächspartnern könnte kaum höher sein. Immer mehr Marken stellen sich daher die Frage, ob es nicht sinnvoller ist, etwas anderes auszuprobieren. So auch der Denimspezialist MUSTANG, der während der Berlin Fashion Week 2017 bewusst auf eine Teilnahme an der Modemesse verzichtete. Stattdessen entwickelte die Modemarke gemeinsam mit DREINULL das „MUSTANG Street Art Lab".

EIN EIGENES STRASSENFEST ALS ENTSPANNTE UND STYLISCHE ALTER- NATIVE ZU VOLLEN MESSEHALLEN.

THEIR OWN STREET FESTIVAL AS A RELAXING AND STYLISH ALTER- NATIVE TO CROWDED EXHIBITION HALLS.

Trade fair exhibitions are interesting contact points with target groups that can otherwise rarely be reached in such a dense and targeted manner. At the same time, attracting the attention of exhibition visitors is no doubt one of the most difficult tasks. The density of stimuli, offers and discussion partners could scarcely be greater. More and more brands are therefore asking themselves whether it would not be more effective to try something else. This was the case for the denim specialist MUSTANG, who deliberately decided not to participate in the fashion fair during the Berlin Fashion Week 2017. Instead, the fashion brand developed the "MUSTANG Street Art Lab" together with DREINULL.

Die SevenStar Gallery in Berlin-Mitte wurde zum zeitlich begrenzten Atelier, Ausstellungsraum und Meeting Place für die Besucher der Berlin Fashion Week, für MUSTANGs wichtigste Einkäufer sowie für alle anderen Modeinteressierten. Künstler wie Clemens Behr, Nomad, SuperBlast und die multidisziplinäre Designerin Jule Waibel waren mit von der Partie. Sie gestalteten vor Ort neue Arbeiten mit den Materialien und Farben der Marke. Tagsüber stand die Galerie offen, abends wurde zum Sundowner mit Drinks, entspannter Musik, neuen Denim-Styles und Live-Performances der Künstler geladen. So gestaltete DREINULL ein alternatives Messeevent, bestehend aus Streetart und Streetwear, das mit steigender Besucherzahl zum eigenen Straßenfest wurde.

The SevenStar Gallery in Berlin-Mitte became a temporary atelier, exhibition space and meeting place for the Berlin Fashion Week visitors, MUSTANG's key buyers, as well as all others interested in fashion. Artists such as Clemens Behr, Nomad, SuperBlast and the multidisciplinary designer Jule Waibel were involved in the event. They designed new works on-site with the materials and colours of the brand. During the daytime the gallery was open, then in the evening guests were invited to a sundowner with drinks, relaxing music, new denim styles and live performances by the artists. DREINULL thus designed an alternative exhibition event, consisting of street art and streetwear, which with increasing numbers of visitors became a street festival in its own right.

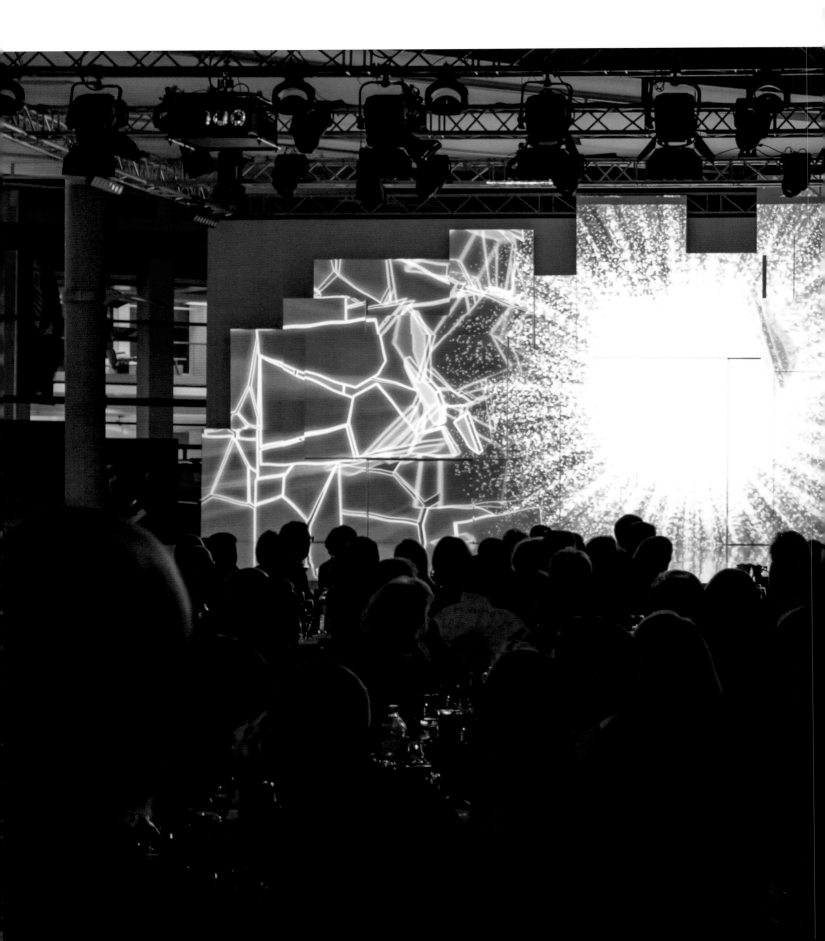

PRESENTATION OF THE NEW MERCEDES-BENZ E-CLASS
PXNG.LI GMBH, KARLSRUHE

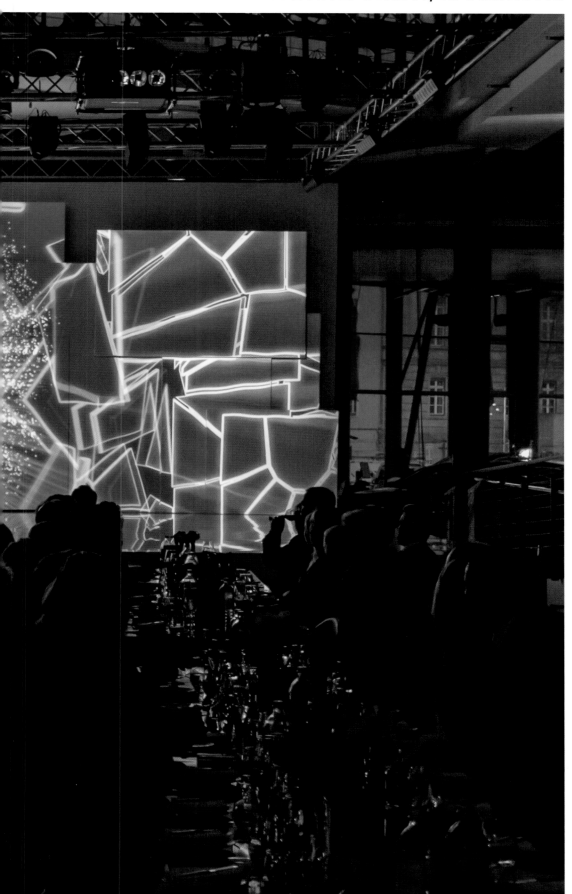

Location
Mercedes-Welt am Salzufer, Berlin

Client
Daimler AG, Berlin

Month / Year
April 2016

Duration
1 day

Dramaturgy / Direction / Coordination / Architecture / Design / Graphics / Lighting / Media / Films / Decoration
PXNG.LI GmbH, Karlsruhe

Music
Musikproduktion Mac Barisch, Karlsruhe

Artists / Show acts
Otto Waalkes und die Friesenjungs, Hamburg

Photos
PXNG.LI GmbH, Karlsruhe;
Dominik Fraßmann, Berlin

A MAPPING SHOW WITH AN ENTERTAINMENT FACTOR AND INFORMATION CONTENT PRESENTED THE NEW E-CLASS.

In April 2016, the new Mercedes E-Class was showcased at the Mercedes-Welt am Salzufer in Berlin under the motto "Masterpiece of Intelligence". As part of a VIP presentation, decisive stages in its history, as well as various high-tech features of the car were to be introduced and explained to the visitors. Apart from the pure entertainment factor, there was therefore also a focus on a high information content. The car was to appear on the stage as part of the show as a dramaturgical highlight.

In der Mercedes-Welt am Salzufer in Berlin wurde im April 2016 die neue Mercedes E-Klasse unter dem Motto „Masterpiece of Intelligence" vorgestellt. Im Rahmen einer VIP-Präsentation sollten entscheidende Etappen der Historie sowie diverse Hightech-Features des Wagens dargestellt und den Besuchern erklärt werden. Neben dem reinen Unterhaltungsfaktor stand somit ein hoher Informationsgehalt im Fokus. Als dramaturgisches Highlight sollte das Auto eingebettet in die Show auf der Bühne erscheinen.

EINE MAPPING-SHOW MIT UNTERHALTUNGSFAKTOR UND INFORMATIONSGEHALT PRÄSENTIERTE DIE NEUE E-KLASSE.

PXNG.LI konzipierte und realisierte mit diesen Zielvorgaben eine Projection-Mapping-Show mit einem Mix aus realen und projizierten Elementen. Die Bühnenrückwand und Projektionsfläche bestand aus mehreren Rechtecken, einer darin eingelassenen Tür sowie einem Garagentor. Die konzipierten Inhalte der Mapping-Show wurden speziell an die Bühne angepasst und sollten mit intelligenten, verblüffenden Effekten überraschen. So war mithilfe unterschiedlicher Mapping-Techniken aus Zuschauersicht kaum noch zwischen projizierten Inhalten und dem real gebauten Raum zu differenzieren. Neben entscheidenden geschichtlichen Etappen und technischen Besonderheiten des Autos wurden die unterschiedlichen Nutzungsräume und -gewohnheiten illustriert. Die Projektionen erzählten unter anderem von Großstadtflair und Vorstadtidyll. Schlussendlich mündete die Präsentation mit dem Öffnen des Garagentors. Der Blick auf die neue E-Klasse wurde frei und das Auto fuhr autonom auf die Bühne.

In accordance with these set goals, PXNG.LI conceived and realised a projection mapping show with a mix of real and projected elements. The rear wall of the stage and projection surface consisted of several rectangles with a door and a garage door set into it. The conceived content of the mapping show was adapted especially to the stage and was designed to surprise the viewers with intelligent, stunning effects. Owing to a variety of mapping techniques, it was scarcely possible from a spectator point of view to distinguish between projected content and real built space. Apart from decisive historical stages and special technical features of the car, the various usage spaces and habits were illustrated. The projections also depicted a city flair and suburban idyll. The presentation finally culminated with the opening of the garage door, revealing the new E-Class car that drove out autonomously onto the stage.

HOTTRENDSXHIBITION
MARBET MARION & BETTINA WÜRTH GMBH & CO. KG, KÜNZELSAU

Location
Motorwerk, Berlin

Client
L'Oréal Deutschland GmbH, Dusseldorf

Month / Year
January 2017

Duration
1 day

Dramaturgy / Direction / Coordination
marbet Marion & Bettina Würth GmbH & Co. KG, Künzelsau

Architecture / Design
marbet Marion & Bettina Würth GmbH & Co. KG; ATELIER KONTRAST GmbH & Co. KG, Heidelberg

Graphics
marbet Marion & Bettina Würth GmbH & Co. KG; flora&faunavisions, Berlin

Media
marbet Marion & Bettina Würth GmbH & Co. KG; flora&faunavisions; Content Cube GmbH, Dusseldorf

Films
marbet Marion & Bettina Würth GmbH & Co. KG; WE OWN YOU, Cologne

Artists / Show acts
marbet Marion & Bettina Würth GmbH & Co. KG; L'Oréal Deutschland GmbH

Decoration
ipoint Messe- und Eventbau GmbH, Schönefeld

Catering
Kofler & Kompanie, Cologne

Photos
Rüdiger Glatz / IMAGE AGENCY, Hamburg

SOCIAL-MEDIA-INHALTE SPANNEN EINEN DRAMATUR-GISCHEN BOGEN VON ONLINE-EINBLICKEN ZUM OFFLINE-EVENT.

Nur selten wird Social Media gezielt und vorab mit dem Konzept eines Events verwoben. Zumeist bleibt es bei einer begleitenden Berichterstattung während des Events. Anders bei der HottrendsXhibition 2017 der Beautymarke Maybelline New York, die im Rahmen der Berlin Fashion Week stattfand. Kerngedanke war es, Kunden, Fans und Follower an der Suche, Inspiration und Entstehung von Trendlooks teilhaben zu lassen. Dafür reiste ein Maybelline Trendsquad, bestehend aus vier Beauty-Bloggern, ein halbes Jahr lang um die Welt – auf der Suche nach den neuesten Beautytrends. YouTube-Trenddokus, Real-Time-Inhalte auf Twitter, inspirierende Fotos und Influencer Takeover auf Instagram sowie Livestreams und Trend-Best-ofs auf Facebook ließen Interessierte an der Reise teilhaben.

It is rare for an event concept to be interwoven with social media in advance in a targeted manner. It is normally limited to accompanying reports during the event. This was not the case for the HottrendsXhibition 2017 by the beauty brand Maybelline New York, which took place as part of Berlin Fashion Week. The core idea was to allow customers, fans and followers to participate in the search, inspiration and creation of trendy looks. For this purpose, a Maybelline trend squad consisting of four beauty bloggers travelled around the world for half a year, searching for the latest beauty trends. YouTube trend documentaries, real-time content on Twitter, inspiring photos and influencer takeovers on Instagram, as well as live streaming and best-of trends on Facebook enabled those interested to take part in the journey.

SOCIAL MEDIA CONTENT FORMS A DRAMATURGICAL BRIDGE BETWEEN ONLINE INSIGHTS AND AN OFFLINE EVENT.

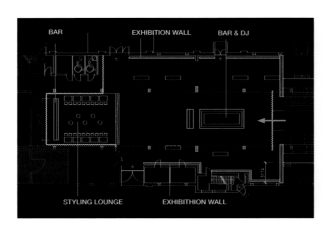

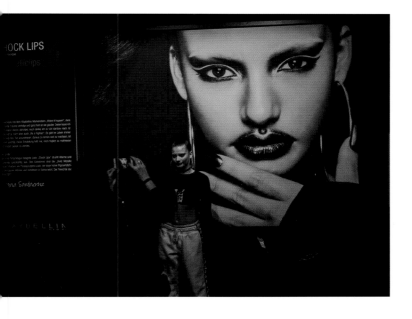

Dramaturgischer Höhepunkt war ein Event mit Runway Show im Rahmen der Berlin Fashion Week – ein multimediales Gesamterlebnis, auf dem die Blogger ihre aufsehenerregendsten Fundstücke der Inspirationsreise präsentierten. Über 300 Quadratmeter Projektionsfläche und eine audiovisuelle Inszenierung setzten die Looks in Szene. Maybelline ergänzte pro Trendlook ein tragbares Everyday Make-up, das vom Trendsquad für ihre Fans übersetzt und abgewandelt wurde. In der HottrendsXhibition wurden die Looks in großformatigen Fotoaufnahmen ausgestellt. So hatten die Gäste im Anschluss die Möglichkeit, sich die Looks im Detail anzuschauen und in der Styling Lounge selbst auszuprobieren.

The dramaturgical highlight was an event with a runway show as part of Berlin Fashion Week – an immersive multimedia event in which the bloggers presented their most sensational finds from the journey of inspiration. Over 300 square metres of projection surface and an audiovisual display set the stage for the looks. Maybelline added wearable everyday makeup for each trendy look, which was applied variously by the trend squad. The looks were exhibited by means of large-scale photographs at the HottrendsXhibition. Guests therefore had the possibility to view the looks in detail afterwards and to try them out themselves in the styling lounge.

#OPELGOESGRUMPY
@GRUMPYSWONDERLAND
VITAMIN E – GESELLSCHAFT FÜR KOMMUNIKATION
MBH, HAMBURG

Location
Kraftwerk Berlin, Berlin

Client
Opel Automobile GmbH, Rüsselsheim a. Main

Month / Year
February 2017

Duration
several days

Dramaturgy
*VITAMIN E – Gesellschaft für
Kommunikation mbH, Hamburg*

Photos
Dirk Dähmlow / diephotodesigner.de, Berlin

EIN INTERNET-PHÄNOMEN WIRD ZUM ROTEN FADEN DER EVENT-INSZENIERUNG UND ZUM MULTIPLIKATOR IN DEN SOZIALEN MEDIEN.

The Opel lifestyle calendar is already quite a tradition for the German car manufacturer. The annual photograph calendar is produced together with varying stars and photographers, as well as human, animal and automobile models. In 2014, Bryan Adams set the stage for the Opel Adam. In 2015, the fashion designer Karl Lagerfeld photographed his cat Choupette around the Opel Corsa. In 2017, the star photographer Ellen von Unwerth depicted Opel car models with the top model Georgia May Jagger and the Internet phenomenon "Grumpy Cat".

Der Opel Lifestyle Kalender ist bereits eine kleine Tradition des deutschen Automobilherstellers. Der jährliche Foto-kalender wird gemeinsam mit wechselnden Stars, Foto-grafen und menschlichen, tierischen sowie automobilen Models produziert. 2014 setzte Bryan Adams den Opel Adam in Szene. 2015 fotografierte Modeschöpfer Karl Lagerfeld seine Katze Choupette im Umfeld des Opel Corsa. 2017 inszenierte Starfotografin Ellen von Unwerth Opel-Auto-modelle mit Topmodel Georgia May Jagger und dem Internetphänomen „Grumpy Cat".

AN INTERNET PHENOMENON BECOMES THE GUIDING THREAD OF THE EVENT STAGING AND A BROADCASTER ON SOCIAL MEDIA.

The publishing of the calendar is always celebrated with a fulminant vernissage. In 2017, VITAMIN E was responsible for the event with more than 1,000 invited guests. Apart from Ellen von Unwerth and Georgia May Jagger, TV stars, bloggers and influencers made their way to the Berlin power plant. Under the guiding theme #OPELGOESGRUMPY @GRUMPYSWONDERLAND, guests immersed themselves in a "cat paradise". The setting included scratching posts, cat food and a cat flap as well as a selfie backdrop with the world-famous cat. A "celebrity roasting" awaited the guests on the red carpet, where the stars had to endure snappy cat comments about themselves. The cat, who was always in a bad mood, also spread her opinion on social media channels, accompanied by photos. The world premiere of the new Opel Crossland X was embedded into the framework of this regular celebrity event.

Die Veröffentlichung des Kalenders wird stets mit einer fulminanten Vernissage gefeiert. 2017 verantwortete VITAMIN E die Veranstaltung für mehr als 1.000 geladene Gäste. Neben Ellen von Unwerth und Georgia May Jagger fanden unter anderem TV-Stars, Blogger und Influencer den Weg ins Berliner Kraftwerk. Unter dem Leitthema #OPELGOESGRUMPY @GRUMPYSWONDERLAND tauchten die Gäste in ein „Katzenparadies" ein. Sowohl Kratzbäume, Katzenfutter und Katzenklappe als auch eine Selfie-Kulisse mit der weltberühmten Katze gehörten zur Inszenierung. Auf dem Roten Teppich erwartete die Gäste ein „Promi-Roasting", bei dem die Stars bissige Katzen-Kommentare über sich ergehen lassen mussten. Begleitet von Fotos verbreitete die stets schlecht gelaunte Katze ihre Meinung auch in den Social-Media-Kanälen. Eingebettet in den Rahmen dieser regelmäßigen Promi-Veranstaltung fand die Weltpremiere des neuen Opel Crossland X statt.

Jede Zielgruppe hat unterschiedliche Bedürfnisse und Erwartungen. Dementsprechend sind Eventkonzepte im Idealfall nicht nur auf den Absender, sondern vor allem auf die Empfänger zugeschnitten.

PRESS: SÄMTLICHE VERTRETER DER MEDIEN, ALSO NATIONALE UND INTERNATIONALE JOUR- NALISTEN (TV, PRINT, RADIO), BLOGGER, INFLUENCER – ALL JENE MULTIPLIKATOREN, DIE DAS SUJET BEHERRSCHEN UND INHALTE GEKONNT WEITER- TRAGEN SOLLEN. DASS BEI DIESER ZIELGRUPPE LIVE- KOMMUNIKATION AN ERSTER STELLE STEHT, IST SELBST- VERSTÄNDLICH ...

Each target group has different requirements and expectations. Event concepts are therefore ideally not only geared towards the addressor, but especially towards the recipients.

PRESS: ALL REPRESENTATIVES OF THE MEDIA, NATIONAL AND INTERNATIONAL JOURNALISTS (TV, PRINT, RADIO), BLOGGERS, INFLUENCERS – ALL THE DISSEMINATORS WHO MASTER THE SUBJECT AND CAN SPREAD CONTENT EXPERTLY. IT GOES WITHOUT SAYING THAT LIVE COMMUNICATION IS KEY WITH THIS TARGET GROUP ...

DAIMLER MEDIA NIGHT IAA
[MU:D] GMBH BÜRO FÜR EREIGNISSE, COLOGNE

Location
Heizkraftwerk Linden, Hanover

Client
Daimler AG, Stuttgart

Month / Year
September 2016

Duration
1 day

**Dramaturgy / Direction / Coordination /
Architecture / Design / Music**
[mu:d] GmbH Büro für Ereignisse, Cologne

Graphics
[mu:d] GmbH Büro für Ereignisse;
FVJ Content Refinery GmbH, Berlin

Lighting
LIGHTCOMPANY GmbH, Neuss

Media
Production Resource GmbH, Hamburg

Films
[mu:d] GmbH Büro für Ereignisse

Decoration
DECOR+MORE Birgit Martinez e.K., Fellbach

Catering
Rauschenberger GmbH & Co. KG, Fellbach

Realisation
Klartext Grafik Messe Event GmbH, Willich

Others
RÖDER Zelt- und Veranstaltungstechnik
GmbH, Büdingen-Wolferborn (Marquee
building); Nüssli Gruppe, Hüttwilen (Stage
facility); laserfabrik GmbH, Hürth (Laser);
Stageco Deutschland GmbH, Königsbrunn
(Special construction trussing)

Photos
Marco Reufzaat, Dusseldorf

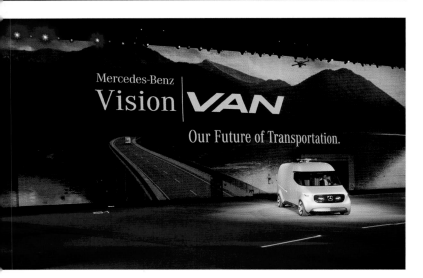

THE LOCATION AS THE CORE OF STORY-TELLING AND THE EFFECTIVE ADVANCE ANNOUNCEMENT OF THE EVENT TO THE PUBLIC.

DIE LOCATION ALS KERN DES STORYTELLINGS UND ÖFFENTLICHKEITS-WIRKSAME VORANKÜNDIGUNG DES EVENTS.

Die Wahl der Location ist ein bedeutender Teil der Event-konzeption, da das räumliche Umfeld maßgeblich zum Storytelling und einem konsistenten Erlebnis beiträgt. Für die „Daimler Media Night IAA 2016" hat sich mu:d daher bewusst für das Kraftwerk Linden entschieden, den Komplex effektvoll eingebunden und über das Event hinaus insze-niert. Das Ziel der Veranstaltung bestand in der Vorkommu-nikation für die Messe IAA Nutzfahrzeuge 2016 in Hannover. Inhaltlicher Höhepunkt war die Weltpremiere des rein elek-trisch betriebenen „Urban eTruck", der zusammen mit dem „Future Bus" und dem „Vision Van" das zukunftsorientierte Trio der Geschäftsbereiche Daimler Trucks, Daimler Buses und Mercedes-Benz Vans bildet. Unter den 500 eingeladenen Gästen waren internationale Journalisten, Medienvertreter von TV-Anstalten und Blogger.

The choice of location is an important aspect of an event concept, as the spatial environment contributes significantly towards the storytelling and a coherent experience. For the "Daimler Media Night IAA 2016", mu:d therefore decided consciously on the Linden power plant. They incorporated the complex to great effect and staged it beyond the event. The aim of the event was to provide advance communication for the IAA Utility Vehicles 2016 exhibition in Hanover. The highlight of the content was the world premiere of the electrically driven "urban e-truck", which – together with the "Future Bus" and the "Vision Van" – forms the pioneering trio of the business areas Daimler Trucks, Daimler Buses and Mercedes-Benz Vans. International journalists, media repre-sentatives from TV companies and bloggers were among the 500 invited guests.

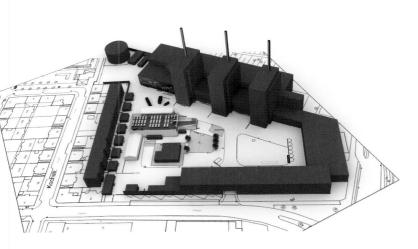

Die drei als Kultobjekt geltenden Kraftwerktürme der Location wurden zum optischen Highlight und essenziellen Teil des Storytellings. Mittels Projektionen wurden die Türme schon vor dem Event als überdimensionale Batterien inszeniert und prägten das nächtliche Stadtbild Hannovers. Täglich erhöhte sich der visualisierte „Akkuladestatus" und kündigte die Veranstaltung öffentlichkeitswirksam an. Die eigentliche Präsentation wurde auf 1.200 Quadratmetern Gebäudewand des Kraftwerks projiziert und mithilfe von Lasereffekten auf dem Boden in eine zweite Dimension überführt. Ein temporärer, gläserner Bau mit Open-Air-Tribüne und urbaner Freitreppe diente als wetterunabhängige Location. So blieben die angestrahlten Türme unverdeckt und die Nähe zum Wahrzeichen des Events und seiner Geschichte erhalten. Zum Finale fuhren die drei Fahrzeuge auf die Szenenfläche und setzten das Schlussbild.

The three power plant towers of the location, regarded as a cult object, became the visual highlight and an essential part of the storytelling. By means of projections, the towers were animated even before the event as oversized batteries and were a distinctive feature of the nightly townscape of Hanover. During the day, the envisaged "accolade status" was intensified and announced the event effectively to the public. The actual presentation was projected onto the 1200-square-metre building wall of the power plant and extended into a second dimension by means of laser effects on the ground. A temporary glass structure with an open-air stage and an urban outdoor staircase served as a location that was independent of the weather. The towers remained uncovered and the proximity to the landmark of the event and its history was preserved. As a finale, the three vehicles drove onto the stage area and formed a concluding image.

PRESS

INTERNATIONAL MEDIA LAUNCH
BMW M5 AND BMW i3s
HAGEN INVENT GMBH & CO. KG, DUSSELDORF

Location
Circuito do Estoril, Estoril; Time Out Market, Lisbon; Centro Ambiental, Lisbon

Client
BMW Group, Munich

Month / Year
November – December 2017

Duration
several weeks

Dramaturgy / Direction / Coordination / Graphics / Realisation
HAGEN INVENT GmbH & Co. KG, Dusseldorf

Lighting / Media
POOLgroup GmbH, Emsdetten

Music / Artists / Show acts
PROvents Service Agentur GmbH, Landsberg a. Lech

Catering
The Ritz Carlton Penha Longa, Sintra

Photos
Mathias Hoffmann, Dusseldorf

Ende 2017 präsentierte BMW erstmals in der Unternehmensgeschichte zwei Produktneuheiten der Submarken BMW i und BMW M gemeinsam: die neuen Modelle BMW M5 und BMW i3s. Zwei verschiedene Fahrzeugmodelle, zwei unterschiedliche Markenwelten, vereint innerhalb eines Launch-Events. Ziel und Herausforderung bestanden darin, beide Autos gleichwertig, aber individuell zu positionieren und der internationalen Fachpresse vorzustellen. HAGEN INVENT entwickelte eine kombinierte Fahrvorstellung, die einerseits den gemeinsamen Markenkern, andererseits die Besonderheiten und Unterschiede aufgriff und inszenierte. In Gruppen à 40 Personen lernten die Gäste die Fahrzeuge bei Testfahrten sowohl auf der Rennstrecke als auch in Lissabon und entlang der Küste kennen.

ZWEI FAHRZEUG-MODELLE, ZWEI SUBMARKEN UND EIN EVENT, BEI DEM GEMEINSAMKEITEN UND BESONDERHEITEN ERLEBBAR WERDEN.

TWO VEHICLE MODELS, TWO SUB-BRANDS AND ONE EVENT WHERE SIMILARITIES AND SPECIAL FEATURES CAN BE EXPERIENCED.

At the end of 2017, for the first time in the company's history, BMW presented two new products of the sub-brands BMW i and BMW M together: the new models BMW M5 and BMW i3s. Two different vehicle models, two different brand worlds, brought together within one launch event. The aim and the challenge were to present both cars equally, whilst positioning each individually and presenting them to international media. HAGEN INVENT developed a combined driving presentation that reflected and staged the shared brand core on the one hand and the special features and differences on the other. In groups of 40 people, the guests got to know the vehicles on test drives, not only on the racing track but also in Lisbon and along the coast.

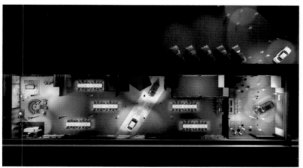

Kernpunkt der Veranstaltung war das physische Aufeinandertreffen von BMW i3s und BMW M5. Unter dem Motto „Brothers in mind – connected through performance" wurden die Produktneuheiten in einer eindrucksvollen Inszenierung auf der Rennstrecke Circuito do Estoril präsentiert. LED Leuchtröhren wurden für die Inszenierung entlang der Tribünen als auch für den Innenausbau der Boxen bei der Abendveranstaltung eingesetzt und vereinten die Lebenswelten der beiden Modelle zu einer gestalterischen Einheit. Zudem wurden beide Neuheiten in ihren individuellen Lebenswelten präsentiert: der BMW i3s im Kontext einer Umwelt- und Nachhaltigkeitsausstellung sowie in hellen, leichten „i Lounges" auf der Rennstrecke; der BMW M5 in seiner ausdrucksstarken, dramatischen schwarz-roten Farbwelt, unter anderem mit einer Heritage-Ausstellung und einem Entertainment-Bereich.

The centrepiece of the event was the physical meeting of the BMW i3s and BMW M5. Under the motto "Brothers in mind – connected through performance", the novel products were presented in an impressive staging on the Circuito do Estoril race track. LED lighting tubes were used for the presentation along the stands, as well as for the interiors of the boxes at the evening event, bringing the worlds of the two models together as a unified design. In addition, the two novelties were presented in their own individual worlds: the BMW i3s in the context of an environment and sustainability exhibition, as well as in light and bright "i Lounges" on the race track, the BMW M5 in its expressive, dramatic, black-red colour world, including with a heritage exhibition and an entertainment area.

AUDI SUMMIT BARCELONA
OETTLE FERBER ASSOCIATES GMBH, GRASBRUNN; CREATORS GMBH, DARMSTADT; DESIGNLIGA GMBH & CO. KG, MUNICH

Location
Gran Via Barcelona, Barcelona

Client
AUDI AG, Ingolstadt

Month / Year
July 2017

Duration
1 day

Architecture / Design
Oettle Ferber Associates GmbH, Grasbrunn

Show concept / Motion graphics
Creators GmbH, Darmstadt

Graphics
Designliga GmbH & Co. KG, Munich
(Graphic design)

Lighting
FOUR TO ONE LIGHTING DESIGN
GMBH, Bornheim (Light planning)

Media
TFN GmbH & Co. KG, Hamburg (Media
planning)

Others
madhat GmbH, Offenbach (Motion graphics /
Staging)

Photos
Audi Media Team / AUDI AG, Ingolstadt

Viele Marken und Unternehmen beschreiten mit alternativen Konzepten neue Pfade abseits von Messepräsenzen. Ein neuartiges, experimentelles Eventformat bildet auch der Audi Summit: Als Alternative zur klassischen Automobilmesse gestalteten Oettle Ferber, Creators und Designliga ein Eventkonzept, das die Stärken von Messe, Konferenz und Show miteinander verbindet. Die Veranstaltung auf einer über 10.000 Quadratmeter großen Fläche richtete sich mit Markeninnovationen und -themen an Presse, Kunden und Influencer.

Many brands and companies tread new paths with alternative concepts beyond for trade fair presences. The Audi Summit also represents a novel, experimental event format: as an alternative to the traditional motor show, Oettle Ferber, Creators and Designliga drew up an event concept that brings together the strengths of a trade fair, conference and show. The event on an area of over 10,000 square metres was targeted towards the media, customers and influencers through brand innovations and themes.

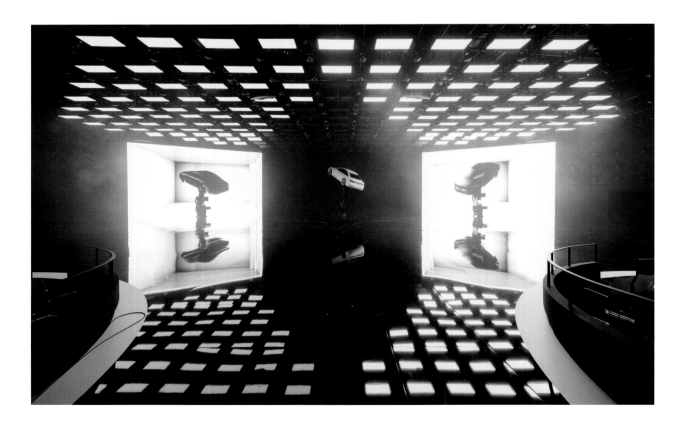

Der Summit gliederte sich in zwei Teile: eine Brandshow im 5.000 Quadratmeter großen Auditorium und einen erlebnis-orientierten Brandspace auf 5.500 Quadratmetern. Die Audi-Summit-Show rückte den Audi A8 als Technologieträger ins Zentrum der Markenpräsentation. Zwischen den Bühnen platziert sollte das Publikum den Wagen und die dynami-sche Fahrzeugshow hautnah miterleben. Das Highlight war die Technologiepräsentation des Audi A8, der sich, auf einen Roboter-Arm montiert, synchron zu den dreidimensionalen Filminhalten bewegte und technische Innovationen impo-sant in Szene setzte.

The summit was divided into two parts: a brand show in the 5000-square-metre auditorium and an experience-orientated brand space of 5500 square metres. The Audi Summit Show placed the Audi A8 as a technology beacon at the centre of the brand presentation. It was positioned between the two stages so that the public could experience the car and the dynamic vehicle show up close. The high-light was the technology presentation of the Audi 8, which was mounted on a robotic arm and moved synchronously with the three-dimensional film content, setting the stage impressively for technical innovations.

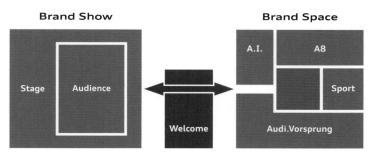

DIE STÄRKEN VON MESSE, KONFERENZ UND SHOW WERDEN ALS EIGENER MARKEN SUMMIT MITEINANDER VERBUNDEN.

Im Anschluss öffneten sich die Tore zum Brandspace. Das Ausstellungskonzept lehnte sich an eine urbane Struktur mit Stadtvierteln und einer zentralen Grünfläche an. Neben moderierten Erlebniszonen, Exponaten und einer Speakers' Corner boten digitale Touchpoints individuelle Informationsmöglichkeiten. Show und Ausstellung waren inhaltlich sowie gestalterisch miteinander verknüpft. So konnten Besucher den Summit nicht nur visuell ganzheitlich erleben, sondern auch Themen der Show innerhalb der Ausstellung vertieft erkunden.

Following on from this, the gates to the brand space opened. The exhibition concept was orientated towards an urban structure with city districts and a central area of greenery. Apart from guided experience zones, exhibits and a Speakers Corner, digital touchpoints offered individual information sources. The show and the exhibition were connected both in terms of content and design. Visitors could therefore not only experience the summit visually as a whole, but also explore the themes of the show in more detail within the exhibition.

THE STRENGTHS OF A TRADE FAIR, CONFERENCE AND SHOW ARE BROUGHT TOGETHER AS A DISTINCTIVE BRAND SUMMIT.

ECANTER FLEET HANDOVER
SIEGELWERK GMBH, STUTTGART

Location
STATION Berlin, Berlin

Client
Daimler AG, Stuttgart

Month / Year
December 2017

Duration
1 day

**Dramaturgy / Direction / Coordination /
Architecture / Design / Graphics / Media**
Siegelwerk GmbH, Stuttgart

Lighting
Neumann&Müller GmbH & Co. KG,
Esslingen a. Neckar

Artists / Show acts
Katharina Garrard, Berlin

Decoration / Realisation
Unit: Art GmbH, Maintal

Catering
Culpepper Event GmbH, Berlin

Photos
Kilian Bishop Fotodesign, Munich

Der Fuso eCanter ist der erste Elektrolastkraftwagen in der Klasse leichter Nutzfahrzeuge. 2017 begann die Auslieferung erster Kleinserien an weltweite Logistikunternehmen. Im Rahmen einer offiziellen Fahrzeugübergabe unter dem Motto „Ready to Deliver – Better Urban Living" erhielten auch vier deutsche Unternehmen die ersten eCanter-Flotten. Der Claim sollte nicht nur die offizielle Einführung des LKWs, sondern auch seinen Beitrag zu Luftqualität und Geräuscharmut im urbanen Raum betonen. Die Verbindung beider Aussagen bildete das gestalterische und dramaturgische Leitmotiv der von Siegelwerk betreuten Veranstaltung.

EINE INSZENIERTE STADT NAMENS „URBANIA" DIENT ALS URBANE KULISSE FÜR DIE ÜBERGABE DER ERSTEN E-LKWS.

A CITY SETTING CALLED "URBANIA" SERVES AS AN URBAN BACKDROP FOR THE HANDOVER OF THE FIRST ELECTRIC LORRIES.

The Fuso eCanter is the first electric lorry in the class of light utility vehicles. 2017 saw the start of the distribution of the first small-scale series to worldwide logistics companies. As part of an official vehicle handover under the motto "Ready to Deliver – Better Urban Living", four German companies also received their first eCanter fleets. The claim was designed not only to highlight the official launch of the vehicle, but also to emphasise its contribution to air quality and lack of noise pollution within the urban area. The combination of both halves of the statement formed the design and dramaturgical key motif of the event conceived by Siegelwerk.

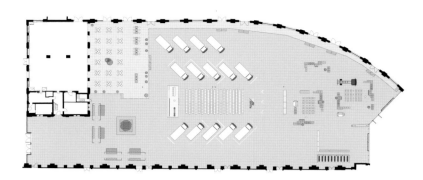

In der Station Berlin, dem ehemaligen Postbahnhof, entstand auf 4.400 Quadratmetern „Urbania" – eine Welt, die das bessere Leben in der Stadt thematisierte. Den Prolog bildete der „Urban Market". In einer Landschaft aus Kartons wurde das Thema „Better Urban Living" aufgegriffen und mit Videoportraits von Berliner Vorzeigeprojekten nähergebracht. Der Hauptteil des Events, die Pressekonferenz, fand im „Product Forum" inmitten der 14 auslieferbereiten Fahrzeuge statt. Für den abschließenden dramaturgischen Höhepunkt setzten sich die LKWs nacheinander in Bewegung. Begleitet von einer E-Violine umkreisten sie die Besucher, bevor sie symbolisch aus der Halle und auf die Straßen deutscher Großstädte ausschwärmten. Die 300 geladenen Journalisten aus Fach- und Lokalpresse konnten im Anschluss in den als urbanen, öffentlichen Platz gestalteten Bereich wechseln und sich bei Street Food austauschen. Der gesonderte Bereich „Wifi Cafe" diente als Rückzugsort, an dem die Gäste in Ruhe einen Kaffee trinken und an den „Working Stations" mit Elektroanschlüssen arbeiten konnten. Den Abschluss des Events bildete eine Party im Berliner Rooftop-Club House of Weekend.

"Urbania" – a world that thematised better urban living – was created on an area of 4400 square metres at the former post train station. The "Urban Market" formed the prologue. The subject of "Better Urban Living" was taken up by a landscape of cardboard boxes and illuminated by video portraits of Berlin showcase projects. The main part of the event, the press conference, was held in the "Product Forum" amidst the 14 vehicles ready for delivery. For the concluding dramaturgical highlight, the vehicles were set in motion one after the other. Accompanied by an electric violin, they circulated the visitors before they swarmed out symbolically from the hall and onto the streets of German cities. The 300 invited journalists from the trade and local press could gather afterwards in the area designed as an urban, public square and converse over street food and lemonade. The separate area "Wi-Fi Café" served as a retreat where guests could drink a coffee in peace and work at the "working stations" with electricity connections. The conclusion to the event was formed by a party at the Berlin Rooftop Club House of Weekend.

"EXPERIENCE AMAZING" –
LEXUS ON-DEMAND PRESS CONFERENCE
VOK DAMS AGENTUR FÜR EVENTS UND
LIVE-MARKETING, WUPPERTAL

Location
Messe Frankfurt, Frankfurt a. Main

Client
Lexus Europe, Brussels

Month / Year
September 2017

Duration
several days

Photos
VOK DAMS Agentur für Events und Live-Marketing, Wuppertal

EINE JEDERZEIT ERLEBBARE MIXED-REALITY-PRESSEKONFERENZ INFORMIERT INDIVIDUELL UND FREI VON TERMINBINDUNGEN.

Pressekonferenzen laufen zumeist nach einem sehr ähnlichen Prinzip ab. Ein offizielles Event informiert eingeladene Journalisten zeitgleich im Rahmen einer Bühnenshow. Die Vorteile eines persönlichen Treffens und gemeinsamen Termins liegen auf der Hand. Doch was ist, wenn Pressevertreter feste Termine nur schwer einhalten können, wie zum Beispiel auf Messen? Um den Journalisten der IAA 2017 mehr zeitliche Flexibilität zu gewähren, entwickelte VOK DAMS eine jederzeit erlebbare Mixed-Reality-Pressekonferenz für die Automobilmarke Lexus.

Press conferences usually follow a very similar principle: an official press event informs invited journalists simultaneously during a stage show. The advantages of the personal encounter and joint time slot are obvious. But what if press representatives find it difficult to keep to fixed deadlines, for example at trade fairs? To give journalists at the IAA 2017 more time flexibility, VOK DAMS developed a mixed reality press conference for the Lexus automotive brand that could be experienced whenever was most convenient.

A MIXED-REALITY PRESS CONFERENCE, WHICH CAN BE EXPERIENCED AT ANY TIME, PROVIDES INDIVIDUAL INFORMATION FREE OF FIXED TIME SLOTS.

Mithilfe der Mixed-Reality-Brille „Microsoft HoloLens" wurde eine 15-minütige interaktive Präsentation gestaltet, die die Journalisten über den Messestand führte. Experten von Lexus begleiteten die Journalisten als Projektion in der Brille und informierten sie über die Modelle und Funktionen. Die Betrachtung der Fahrzeuge und Exponate wurde mit Redebeiträgen, Grafiken, 3D-Animationen, kurzen Video-Einspielungen und Mapping auf den Fahrzeugen erweitert. Ergänzende Reden von Lexus-Europachef Alain Uyttenhoven und den Lexus-Produktspezialisten konnten ebenfalls im virtuellen Sichtfeld der Journalisten angeschaut werden.

Using the mixed-reality glasses "Microsoft HoloLens", a 15-minute interactive presentation was created, which guided the journalists around the exhibition stand. Experts from Lexus, which were projected into the glasses, accompanied the journalists and informed them about the exhibited models and their functions. The viewing of the vehicles and exhibits was supplemented by speeches, graphics, 3D animations, short video recordings and mapping on the vehicles. Additional speeches by the European head of Lexus Alain Uyttenhoven and Lexus product specialists rounded off the individual press conferences in the journalists' virtual field of vision.

THE ALL-NEW POLO
STAGG & FRIENDS GMBH, DUSSELDORF;
DC DESIGNCOMPANY GMBH, MUNICH

Location
Schulauer Fährhafen, Wedel / Hamburg

Client
Volkswagen AG, Wolfsburg

Month / Year
August – September 2017

Duration
several days

Direction / Coordination
STAGG & FRIENDS GmbH, Dusseldorf

Architecture / Design / Graphics
dc designcompany gmbh, Munich

Lighting / Media / Films
TFN GmbH & Co. KG, Hamburg

Decoration
Uschi König / König Styling, Pentenried

Catering
Kofler & Kompanie, Hamburg

Realisation
maedebach werbung gmbh, Brunswick

Photos
Volkswagen AG, Wolfsburg

Im Herbst 2017 gewährte Volkswagen ausgewählten internationalen Journalisten, Bloggern und Influencern einen exklusiven Blick auf den neuen Polo. Wesentliche Kommunikationsziele waren das emotionale Design, die innovative Technik und die umfangreiche Konnektivität sowie die vielfältigen Individualisierungsmöglichkeiten des neuen Modells. Dazu sollte eine originelle, junge, variable und funktionale Location für einen flexiblen Eventablauf gestaltet werden.

In autumn 2017, Volkswagen granted selected international journalists, bloggers and influencers an exclusive viewing of the new Polo. The key communication objectives were emotional design, innovative technology and comprehensive connectivity, as well as the wide range of individualisation possibilities of the new model. The aim was to design an original, young, variable and functional location for the unfolding of a flexible event.

INDIVIDUALISIERUNG ALS GESTALTERISCHER MASSSTAB – UMGESETZT ALS BUNTE, JUNGE UND FLEXIBLE CONTAINERLOCATION.

INDIVIDUALISATION AS A DESIGN BENCHMARK – REALISED AS A COLOURFUL, YOUNG AND FLEXIBLE CONTAINER LOCATION.

STAGG & FRIENDS kreierte gemeinsam mit der dc design-company gmbH ein Konzept, das bunt, zielgruppenorientiert und individuell in den neu erbauten Schulauer Hafen direkt an der Elbe eingebettet wurde. Ausrangierte Schiffscontainer wurden recycelt, in U-Form angeordnet und als unkonventionelle Location ausgebaut. Als „Relaisstation" bildete sie das Herzstück der Veranstaltung, das die Gäste mit den Polo-Testfahrzeugen erreichen konnten. Eine offene und multifunktionale Raumarchitektur, stylisches und farbenfrohes Mobiliar und zwanglos, aber informativ gestaltete Themen- und Informationsbereiche setzten Akzente und schufen eine zu den Kommunikationszielen passende Atmosphäre: jung, frisch, flexibel und kreativ. Mit Blick auf die vorbeiziehenden Containerschiffe konnten die insgesamt rund 500 Gäste das neue Fahrzeug in seiner Vielfalt kennenlernen und in entspannter Umgebung Expertengespräche führen.

STAGG & FRIENDS, together with dc designcompany gmbh, created a colourful, targeted and individual concept incorporated into the newly built Schulauer Hafen right by the Elbe. Discarded ship containers were recycled, arranged in a U-shape and developed into an unconventional event location. As a "relay station", it formed the centrepiece of the event, which the guests could get to with the Polo test vehicles. An open and multifunctional spatial architecture, stylish and colourful furniture and casual, but informatively orientated theme and information areas set accents and created an atmosphere that was commensurate with the communication goals: young, fresh, flexible and creative. With a view of the passing container ships, the total of around 500 guests were able to get to know the new vehicle in all its diversity and hold expert discussions in relaxed surroundings.

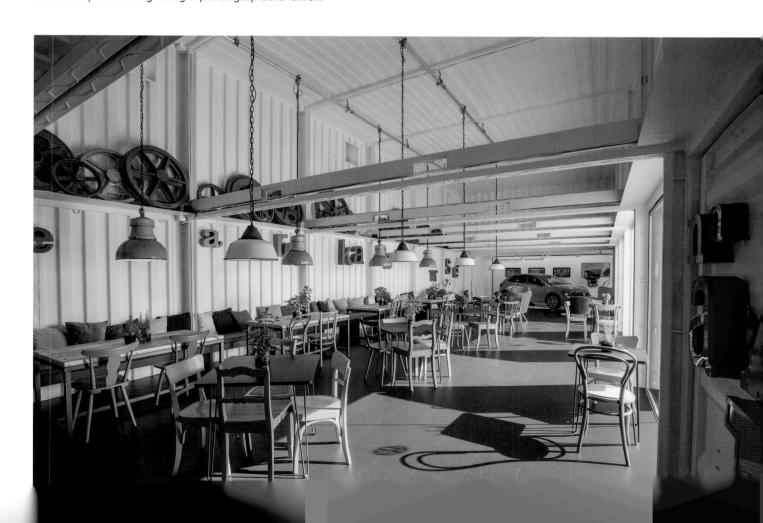

Jede Zielgruppe hat unterschiedliche Bedürfnisse und Erwartungen. Dementsprechend sind Eventkonzepte im Idealfall nicht nur auf den Absender, sondern vor allem auf die Empfänger zugeschnitten.

EMPLOYEES: MITARBEITER EINES ODER MEHRERER UNTERNEHMEN, DIE ZUMEIST MOTIVIERT, ZUSAMMEN-GESCHWEISST ODER GRUND-SÄTZLICH BESSER GESTIMMT WERDEN SOLLEN. DIESE ZIELGRUPPE BEDARF EINES BESONDEREN FEINGEFÜHLS, UM DIE ZIELVORGABEN DES MANAGEMENTS MIT DER EMOTIONALEN WAHRNEHMUNG DER MITARBEITER ZU VEREIN-BAREN UND DIE BEABSICHTIGTE BOTSCHAFT ZU KOMMUNIZIEREN.

Each target group has different requirements and expectations. Event concepts are therefore ideally not only geared towards the addressor, but especially towards the recipients.

EMPLOYEES: EMPLOYEES FROM ONE OR MORE COMPANIES WHO ARE USUALLY TO BE MOTIVATED, BROUGHT TOGETHER OR GENERALLY HAVE THEIR SPIRITS RAISED. THIS TARGET GROUP REQUIRES A SPECIAL TOUCH IN ORDER TO ALIGN THE AIMS OF THE MANAGEMENT WITH THE EMOTIONAL PERCEPTION OF THE EMPLOYEES AND TO COMMUNICATE THE INTENDED MESSAGE.

DIGITALLIFE DAY
PULSMACHER GMBH, LUDWIGSBURG

Location
Werkzentrum Weststadt, Ludwigsburg

Client
Daimler AG, Stuttgart

Month / Year
May 2017

Duration
1 day

**Direction / Coordination / Architecture /
Design / Graphics**
pulsmacher GmbH, Ludwigsburg

Lighting
Lautmacher GmbH, Ludwigsburg

Catering
Schräglage GmbH, Stuttgart

Realisation
bluepool GmbH, Leinfelden-Echterdingen

Photos
Christopher Kreymborg, Stuttgart

Im Mai 2017 lud die Daimler AG 1.000 ihrer Mitarbeiter zum eintägigen DigitalLife Day – ein an ein Festival angelehntes Eventformat, das den Freiraum für frische Ideen und Austausch schaffen sollte. Kernthema war der digitale Wandel und seine Folgen für das digitale Leben. Als raumbildende Elemente dienten Baugerüste, die das 3.500 Quadratmeter große Gelände strukturieren und gleichzeitig die angestrebte Innovationskultur des Unternehmens greifbar machen sollten.

EIN UNGEZWUN-GENES FESTIVAL ALS JÄHRLICH WIEDERKEHRENDER ORT FÜR NEUE IDEEN UND VERÄNDERUNG.

A CASUAL FESTIVAL AS AN ANNUALLY RECURRING PLACE FOR NEW IDEAS AND CHANGE.

In May 2017, Daimler AG invited 1,000 of their employees to attend the one-day DigitalLife Day – an event format evoking a festival, which was designed to create a space for fresh ideas and exchanges. The core topic was digital transformation and its consequences for digital life. Scaffolding served as spatial structuring elements for the 3,500-square-metre site and at the same time the purpose of making the striven for innovation culture of the company tangible.

Inhaltlich boten vier Bühnen mit den Schwerpunkten „transform", „ideate", „collaborate" und „change" Podiumsdiskussionen und Talks mit rund 40 internen wie externen Rednern. An unterschiedlichen Stationen wurden neue Ideen und Produkte persönlich und unmittelbar vorgestellt. Der „IdeationJungle" bot kreativen Teams, die durch das virtuelle Crowdfunding der Daimler AG gefördert werden sollten, Platz für die Vorbereitung ihrer Pitch Präsentationen. Festivalelemente wie Entertainment- und Entspannungsbereiche lockerten das inhaltliche Programm auf und luden unter anderem im Festival-Look gestalteten Außenbereich zu Gesprächen in ungezwungener Atmosphäre ein. Die Teilnehmer konnten sich dabei frei zwischen allen Programmpunkten nach Lust und Interesse entscheiden. Auf ein Pflichtprogramm verzichtete die betreuende Agentur pulsmacher ganz bewusst. Ein Highlight des Tages war der Talk mit dem Vorstandsvorsitzenden Dieter Zetsche, in dem klar wurde: Die motivierten Mitarbeiter möchten auch weiterhin maßgeblich an Weiterentwicklungen, Veränderungen und zukunftsweisenden Ideen beteiligt sein. Auch 2018 wird es einen DigitalLife Day geben, der sich zum Ziel setzt, einen Ort dafür zu schaffen.

In terms of content, four stages with a respective focus on "transform", "ideate", "collaborate" and "change" offered podium discussions and talks with around 40 internal and external speakers. New ideas and products were presented personally and directly at the different stations. The „Ideation Jungle" offered creative teams who were to be sponsored by the virtual crowdfunding of Daimler AG space to prepare their pitch presentations. Festival elements such as entertainment and relaxation areas lightened up the content programme and invited discussions in a casual atmosphere, including in the outdoor area designed with a festival look. The participants could choose freely between all the programme points as they pleased and according to their interests. The responsible agency pulsmacher avoided an obligatory programme quite deliberately. A highlight of the day was the talk with the chairman Dieter Zetsche, in which it became clear that the motivated employees wish to continue being significantly involved in further development, change and forward-looking ideas. There will be a further DigitalLife Day in 2018, with the aim of creating a forum for that.

COVESTRO INNOVATION CELEBRATION EMEA
INSGLÜCK GESELLSCHAFT FÜR MARKENINSZENIERUNG MBH, BERLIN

Location
X-Post, Cologne

Client
Covestro Deutschland AG, Leverkusen

Month / Year
July 2017

Duration
1 day

Dramaturgy / Direction / Coordination / Architecture / Design / Graphics / Media
insglück Gesellschaft für Markeninszenierung mbH, Berlin

Lighting / Music
Neumann&Müller Gmbh & Co. KG, Dusseldorf

Decoration
BALLONI GmbH, Cologne

Catering
Kofler & Kompanie, Cologne

Others
timpact GmbH, Berlin (Coaching)

Photos
Fotograf Rennertz, Meerbusch

MITARBEITER WERDEN INHALTLICH SOWIE SYMBOLISCH ZU GESTALTERN. DAS EINZIGE VISUELLE MITTEL: FARBE.

Innovationen kann man nicht einfach erwarten, man muss sie fördern und feiern. In diesem Sinne bringt Covestro als Anbieter für Polymerwerkstoffe jährlich seine internationalen Mitarbeiter zu einer „Innovation Celebration" zusammen. Forschungs- und Innovationsprojekte werden nicht nur präsentiert, sondern in Workshops wird auch gemeinsam an ihnen gearbeitet und letztlich so das Networking und Zusammengehörigkeitsgefühl gestärkt. Für die Veranstaltung im Jahr 2017 entwickelte insglück ein farbenfrohes, inter- aktives Konzept, das aus der Marke sowie aus dem Postulat „curious, couragous and colourful" entsprungen ist.

You cannot just expect innovation, it must be fostered and celebrated. This is the spirit in which Covestro, a supplier of polymer materials, brings its international employees to- gether every year for an "Innovation Celebration". Research and innovation projects are not just presented, but worked on together in workshops, strengthening networking and a sense of community. For the event in 2017, insglück deve- loped a richly colourful, interactive concept that emerged from the brand and the postulate "curious, courageous and colourful".

EMPLOYEES BECOME DESIGNERS BOTH SYMBOLICALLY AND IN TERMS OF CONTENT. THE ONLY VISUAL MEANS: COLOUR.

Das Motto „White Wall – Colour Your Space" brachte das Veranstaltungsziel auf den Punkt: Die Mitarbeiter sollten im wörtlichen Sinne die weißen Wände mit bunten Ideen füllen. Mit Regencapes bekleidet durften die 500 Gäste zum Warm-up die weiße Bühnenrückwand mit aufwendig produzierten Farbeiern bewerfen und ein starkes Sinnbild erschaffen. Das gesamte Raumdesign folgte diesem Ansatz mit vielen weißen Flächen und gezielten, bunten Farbakzenten. Inhaltlich erwartete die Teilnehmer eine Vielzahl interaktiver und mehrstufiger Maßnahmen. Schon vor dem Event konnten die Mitarbeiter über ein Portal Themen und Workshops mitgestalten. Das gleiche Portal bot die Möglichkeit, sich mit eigenen Ideen bei einer hochdotierten Start-up-Challenge zu bewerben. Nach einem ausführlichen Coaching präsentierten 15 Finalisten ihre Ideen auf dem Event in einem Pecha-Kucha-Format, bevor die Gewinner als Highlight des Tages gekürt wurden. Ein Sticker-Tausch-Album mit allen eingereichten Projekten und ihren Teams sorgte für zusätzliche Networking-Anreize.

The motto "White Wall – Colour Your Space" put the objective of the event in a nutshell: the employees were literally to fill the white walls with colourful ideas. Wearing rain capes, the 500 guests were invited to throw elaborately produced coloured eggs at the white rear wall of the stage as a warm-up, creating a powerful image. The whole spatial design followed this principle, with many white surfaces and a targeted array of colour accents. In terms of content, a range of interactive and multi-stage measures awaited the participants. Already before the event, the employees were able to contribute to themes and workshops through a portal. The same portal offered the possibility to submit their own ideas to a highly rewarded start-up challenge. After extensive coaching, the 15 finalists presented their ideas at the event in a Pecha Kucha format, before the winners were announced as the highlight of the day. A sticker album with all the submitted projects and their teams provided additional networking impulses.

LEADERSHIP 2020 SUMMIT
[MU:D] GMBH BÜRO FÜR EREIGNISSE, COLOGNE

Location
FREDENHAGEN, Offenbach a. Main

Client
Daimler AG, Stuttgart

Month / Year
May 2017

Duration
several days

Dramaturgy / Direction / Coordination / Architecture / Design / Music
[mu:d] GmbH Büro für Ereignisse, Cologne

Graphics
[mu:d] GmbH Büro für Ereignisse;
VON HELDEN UND GESTALTEN GmbH,
Stuttgart

Lighting / Media
Production Resource Group AG, Hamburg

Films
VON HELDEN UND GESTALTEN GmbH

Decoration
DECOR+MORE Birgit Martinez e.K., Fellbach

Catering
Gauls Catering GmbH & Co. KG, Mainz

Realisation
Klartext Grafik Messe Event GmbH, Willich

Photos
Stephan Brendgen, Monheim; Stephanie
Trenz, Stuttgart

Ob neue Technologien oder die Individualisierung – für Unternehmen gehen diese vielfältigen Entwicklungen mit einem neuen Führungsverständnis einher. So hat auch Daimler sich zum Ziel gesetzt, eine neue Führungskultur mit acht neuen Führungsprinzipien zu etablieren. Zentraler Baustein der dazugehörigen Change-Strategie war der Leadership Summit 2020 unter dem Motto „Change the Game". mu:d konzipierte hierfür ein mehrstufiges Event, das die 1.300 Teilnehmer weiterbilden und emotional auf die neuen Prinzipien einschwören sollte. Als dramaturgischer Leitfaden diente der Hashtag #stepintochange. Im ersten „Schritt" konnten sich alle Daimler-Mitarbeiter über ein Online-Verfahren um eine Teilnahme bei dem Event bewerben. Ein Online-Tool informierte vorab über das Programm und ermöglichte die Zusammenstellung einer individuellen Agenda. Als emotionale Einstimmung und Unterstützung erhielt jeder Teilnehmer Change-the-Game-Sneaker in den Corporate-Design-Farben der Kampagne – „Schritt" Nummer zwei. Die darauf folgende eine WHY-Box visualisierte in einer 360°-Projektion den Daimler-Pioniergeist sowie die Herausforderungen des neuen Zeitalters. Zugleich symbolisierte sie den dritten „Schritt".

Whether it is new technologies or individualisation – for companies, these wide-ranging developments go hand in hand with a new understanding of leadership. Daimler therefore also set itself the goal of establishing a new leadership culture through eight new leadership principles. The central building block of the subsequent strategy of change was the Leadership Summit 2020 under the motto "Change the Game". A multi-tiered event was designed by mu:d for this purpose, to inaugurate the new principles and prepare the 1,300 participants for them emotionally. The hashtag #stepintochange served as a dramaturgical thread. As a first "step", all Daimler employees could apply to participate in the event via an online procedure. An online tool provided advance information about the programme and enabled an individual agenda to be put together. To tune the participants in emotionally and as a support during the first steps, each received a Change the Game sneaker in the corporate design colours of the campaign – "step" two. The ensuing WHY Box visualised the Daimler pioneering spirit and the challenges of the new era in a 360° projection. At the same time, it symbolised the third "step".

LEADERSHIP SUMMIT 2020 – THE FIRST LITERALLY QUIET STEPS TOWARDS A NEW LEADERSHIP CULTURE.

LEADERSHIP SUMMIT 2020 – DIE ERSTEN, IM WÖRTLICHEN SINNE RUHIGEN SCHRITTE HIN ZUR NEUEN FÜHRUNGSKULTUR.

The summit was opened in a fourth and final "step". The design concept of the summit event area reflected the leadership principles and served as an open platform for the programme, with modules from infotainment and entertainment. The plenum, Speakers' Corner and eight of the total of 16 workshops were carried out as a silent conference, allowing the creation of a quiet atmosphere with large, connecting spaces and wide visual axes. The programme was transmitted live on the Daimler social media platform and made accessible to all employees around the world.

Mit dem vierten und letzten „Schritt" wurde der Summit eröffnet. Das Designkonzept der Summit-Event-Area spiegelte die Führungsprinzipien und diente dem Programm als offene Plattform mit Modulen aus Info- und Entertainment. Plenum, Speakers' Corner und acht der insgesamt 16 Workshops wurden als Silent-Konferenz durchgeführt, wodurch eine ruhige Atmosphäre mit großen, verbindenden Räumen und weiten Sichtachsen geschaffen wurde. Das Programm wurde live auf der Daimler-Social-Media-Plattform übertragen und allen Mitarbeitern weltweit zugänglich gemacht.

Jede Zielgruppe hat unterschiedliche Bedürfnisse und Erwartungen. Dementsprechend sind Eventkonzepte im Idealfall nicht nur auf den Absender, sondern vor allem auf die Empfänger zugeschnitten.

EXPERTS: FACHPUBLIKUM, BRANCHENKENNER UND EXPERTEN, DIE AN EINEM GEMEINSAMEN THEMA INTERESSIERT SIND. DER AUSTAUSCH AUF FACHEBENE STEHT DABEI IM MITTELPUNKT UND PRÄGT DIE KOMMUNIKATION WESENTLICH. DIESE ZIELGRUPPE IST VORNEHMLICH AN DER VERMITTLUNG VON WISSEN INTERESSIERT, DIE WEIT ÜBER DIE WEITERGABE REINER INFORMATIONEN HINAUSGEHT.

Each target group has different requirements and expectations. Event concepts are therefore ideally not only geared towards the addressor, but especially towards the recipients.

EXPERTS: THESE ARE A SPECIALIST PUBLIC AND EXPERTS IN THE SECTOR WHO ARE INTERESTED IN A COMMON SUBJECT. THE FOCUS IS ON AN EXCHANGE AT EXPERT LEVEL, WHICH SHAPES THE COMMUNICATION SIGNIFICANTLY. THIS TARGET GROUP IS PRIMARILY INTERESTED IN THE TRANSMISSION OF KNOWLEDGE THAT GOES WAY BEYOND THE PASSING ON OF MERE INFORMATION.

FAMAB AWARD
JAZZUNIQUE GMBH, FRANKFURT A. MAIN

Location
Forum am Schlosspark, Ludwigsburg

Client
FAMAB e.V., Rheda-Wiedenbrück

Month / Year
November 2017

Duration
1 day

Dramaturgy / Direction / Coordination
Jochen Hinken, Emsdetten

Architecture / Design
Jazzunique GmbH, Frankfurt a. Main

Lighting
BJÖRN HERMANN lichtdesign, Berlin

Media
congaz Visual Media Company GmbH,
Dusseldorf

Realisation
jungbauten GmbH, Augsburg

Others
Kaiser Showtechnik, Augsburg (Light /
sound / kinetics); Media Resource Group
GmbH & Co. KG, Crailsheim (Video / LED);
Screen Visions GmbH, Stuttgart (LED walls);
epicto GmbH, Edingen-Neckarhausen (LED
walls); Lichtfaktor GmbH, Cologne (Light art
performance); MH Production, Gütersloh
(Technical direction)

Photos
Börries Götsch / Jazzunique GmbH, Frankfurt a. Main; Sandra Sommerkamp, Munich

Die Konzeption und Gestaltung von Bühnendesigns birgt nicht selten mehr Herausforderungen als zunächst gedacht. Sowohl eine ausdrucksstarke Wirkung als auch die individuelle Funktion müssen präzise umgesetzt werden. Schwächen fallen bei den zumeist langen Betrachtungszeiten schnell auf. Im Fall des jährlich verliehenen Preises der Eventbranche, dem FAMAB Award, galt es, die Nominierten unter Berücksichtigung des knappen Zeitfensters zu inszenieren und gleichzeitig eine geeignete Präsentationsfläche für die Award-Filme zu schaffen.

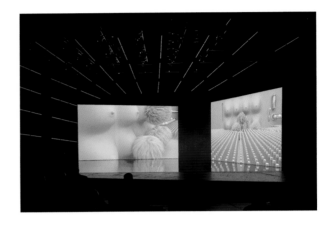

RAUMTIEFE UND MINIMALISMUS SORGEN FÜR SPANNENDE PERSPEKTIVEN UND STELLEN DIE INHALTE IN DEN FOKUS.

The concept and creation of stage designs often harbour greater challenges than initially expected. Both an expressive effect and the individual function must be precisely realised. Any weaknesses are soon noticed, as they are usually the focus of attention for a lengthy period. In the case of the annually awarded prize in the events sector, the FAMAB Award, it was about staging the nominees within the narrow time window available and at the same time creating a suitable presentation surface for the award films.

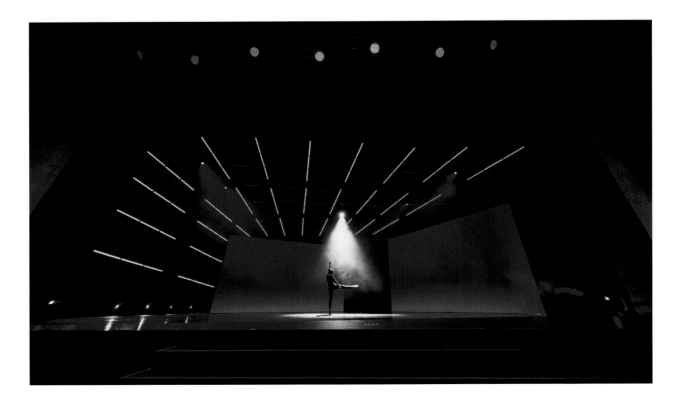

SPATIAL DEPTH AND MINIMALISM PROVIDE EXCITING PERSPECTIVES AND PLACE A FOCUS ON CONTENT.

For the two main requirements, Jazzunique 2017 used the whole depth of the stage area. Two screens positioned freely in the space, combined with a mirrored area on the floor, provided additional visual depth and unusual perspectives. Depending on the sitting position of the spectator, various stage impressions were created. Artistic media content by Congaz and the lighting design by Björn Hermann completed the modest design. The minimalist, but effective approach allowed the creation of a new space for each programme point.

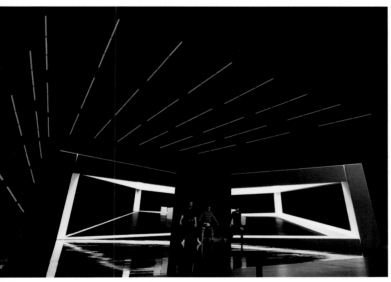

Für die beiden Hauptansprüche nutzte Jazzunique 2017 die gesamte Tiefe des Bühnenraums. Zwei frei im Raum positionierte Screens, kombiniert mit einer Spiegelfläche auf dem Boden, sorgten für zusätzliche visuelle Tiefe und ungewöhnliche Perspektiven. Abhängig vom Sitzplatz des Zuschauers entstanden unterschiedliche Bühneneindrücke. Künstlerischer Mediencontent von congaz und das Lichtdesign von Björn Hermann komplettierten die zurückhaltende Gestaltung. Der minimalistische, aber effektvolle Ansatz ermöglichte es, für jeden Programmpunkt einen neuen Raum zu erschaffen.

C-HR BERLIN INNOVATION & CREATIVITY FESTIVAL

MARBET MARION & BETTINA WÜRTH GMBH & CO. KG, KÜNZELSAU; POPULAR GROUP, HAMBURG

Location
Kaufhaus Jandorf, Berlin

Client
Toyota Deutschland GmbH, Cologne

Month / Year
October 2016

Duration
several days

Dramaturgy / Graphics / Films / Artists / Show acts
marbet Marion & Bettina Würth GmbH & Co. KG, Künzelsau; POPULAR GROUP, Hamburg

Direction / Coordination
marbet Marion & Bettina Würth GmbH & Co. KG

Architecture / Design
marbet Marion & Bettina Würth GmbH & Co. KG; ATELIER KONTRAST, Heidelberg

Media
marbet Marion & Bettina Würth GmbH & Co. KG; flora&faunavisions, Berlin; Affenfaust Galerie, Hamburg; VR Nerds GmbH, Hamburg

Decoration
ipoint Messe- und Eventbau GmbH, Schönefeld

Catering
Bpuls Event & Catering GmbH, Berlin; The Bowl, Berlin

Photos
Tom Woollard, Yorkshire

EIN EIGENES INNOVATION & CREATIVITY FESTIVAL STATT KLASSISCHER PRODUKTEINFÜHRUNG.

Mit klassischen Markteinführungsevents, bei denen alleine das Produkt im Mittelpunkt steht, kann die junge Zielgruppe immer seltener erreicht werden. Marken brauchen den Mut, neue Wege der Markenführung und -kommunikation aus- zuprobieren. Dazu gehört auch, sich ein Stück weit von der Zentrierung des eigenen Produkts zu lösen. So wird verständ- lich, warum Toyota sich anlässlich der Markteinführung des C-HR für ein zweiwöchiges, interdisziplinäres Festival rund um Kunst, Design, Fashion und Digitalisierung entschied. Wissbegierige Pioniere, Gründer, Künstler, Musiker, Designer und Fashionistas gehörten zur Zielgruppe des von marbet gestalteten Events. Sie waren eingeladen, im umgestalteten Kaufhaus Jandorf in Berlin-Mitte auf innovative Vordenker aus aller Welt zu treffen. Einblicke in internationale, außergewöhn- liche Projekte und inspirierender Ideenaustausch sollten zu dieser untypischen Markteinführungskampagne locken.

With classical market launch events that focus on the product alone it is increasingly difficult to reach the young target group. Brands need the courage to try out new ways of brand presentation and communication. This also includes stepping back a little from a central focus on one's own product. This explains why Toyota decided on a two-week interdisciplinary festival comprising art, design, fashion and digitisation, on the occasion of the market launch of the C-HR. Pioneers, founders, artists, musicians, designers and fashionistas eager for knowledge were among the target group for the event designed by marbet. They were invited to meet innovative forward thinkers from around the world at the converted department store Jandorf in Berlin-Mitte. Insights into the exceptional international projects and an inspiring exchange of ideas were intended to entice the visitors to this atypical market launch campaign.

In Workshops und Vorträgen informierten Trainer über Themen wie Design, Technik, Fashion, Nachhaltigkeit und Innovation. Kunst-, Design- und Fashionpräsentationen ergänzten das inhaltliche Programm. Aus kulinarischer Sicht spiegelte junge, frische Küche in einer Pop-up-Kantine, einer Bar sowie einem Café die Inhalte. Der eigene Co-Working-Space ermöglichte es den Teilnehmern, zwischendurch zu arbeiten. Anregende Impulse gab es in zwei Tilt-Brush-360°-VR-Experience-Arenen, einem Sounddesign-Studio und der Projektinstallation „Overflow". Eine 8 × 6 Meter große Lichtinstallation mit dem Titel „Paradise Baby" trug zur räumlichen Atmosphäre bei. Begleitet wurde das Festival durch die Kommunikation in verschiedenen Social-Media-Kanälen.

In workshops and talks, trainers provided information about topics such as design, technology, fashion, sustainability and innovation. Art, design and fashion presentations supplemented the programme content. From a culinary point of view, the content was reflected in young, fresh cuisine in a pop-up canteen, a bar and a café. The co-working space allowed participants to work in between times. Stimulating impulses were provided by two Tilt Brush 360° VR experience arenas, a sound design studio and the project installation "Overflow". An 8 × 6-metre lighting installation with the title "Paradise Baby" contributed to the spatial atmosphere. The festival was accompanied by communication in various social media channels.

AN IDIOSYNCRATIC INNOVATION & CREATIVITY FESTIVAL INSTEAD OF A CLASSICAL PRODUCT LAUNCH.

100 YEARS ANNIVERSARY ME ELECMETAL
CQ ESTUDIO, SANTIAGO

Location
Casa Piedra, Santiago

Client
ME Elecmetal, Santiago

Month / Year
October 2017

Duration
1 day

Dramaturgy / Direction / Coordination / Architecture / Design / Graphics / Lighting / Decoration / Realisation
CQ Estudio, Santiago

Production
CPC corporate events, Santiago

Media
CQ Estudio; ME Elecmetal

Films
CQ Estudio; PI proyección de ideas, Santiago; Daf, Santiago

Music / Artists / Show acts
Hugo Manzi, Santiago

Catering
Casa Piedra, Santiago

Photos
Gustavo Zambra, Santiago

Im Jahr 2017 wurde das Unternehmen ME Elecmetal 100 Jahre alt – ein Meilenstein, der mit Kunden, Lieferanten, Mitarbeitern und Shareholdern gefeiert werden sollte. Ziel war ein inspirierendes und dynamisches Ereignis mit einer Reise durch die Vergangenheit, Gegenwart und Zukunft des Unternehmens. Zusammen mit den inhaltlichen Anforderungen nutzte CQ Estudio die Produkte der Firma – unter anderem Schmelzöfen und Mahlanlagen – als gestalterischen Ausgangspunkt. Entsprechend der inhaltlichen Etappen wurde das Event in drei Räume unterteilt.

In the year 2017, the company ME Elecmetal turned 100 years old – a milestone that was to be celebrated with customers, suppliers, employees and shareholders. The aim was to create an inspiring and dynamic event involving a journey through the past, present and future of the company. Together with the content requirements, CQ Estudio used the products of the company – including smelting furnaces and grinding systems – as a starting point for the design. In accordance with the stages of the content, the event was divided into three spaces.

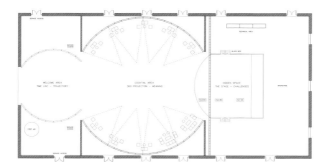

A JOURNEY THROUGH THE PAST, PRESENT AND FUTURE AS A SPATIAL-DRAMATURGICAL EVENT.

Der erste Raum diente der Begrüßung und dramaturgischen Einleitung. Hier wurden die wichtigsten, archivierten Meilensteine und Anekdoten von ME Elecmetal anhand einer groß angelegten Zeitleiste, wie man sie etwa aus Museen kennt, vorgestellt. Der darauf folgende Raum ergänzte die Zeitleiste mit einer 360°-Projektion. Zu sehen waren die wichtigsten Fakten der entwickelten Innovationen und neuen Technologien. Nach den Reden der Gastgeber untermalte ein projiziertes Video die Bedeutung und Verantwortung, die aus dem 100-jährigen Bestehen hervorgehen. Der dritte Raum, der die zukünftigen Herausforderungen musikalisch symbolisierte, blieb bis zum Schluss verborgen. Eine Fusion aus klassischen Instrumenten und zeitgenössischen, elektronischen Sounds versinnbildlichte die Vergangenheit, Gegenwart und Zukunft als zusammenhängende Einheit – und bildete den dramaturgischen Höhepunkt der Veranstaltung. Die für den Eingangsbereich gestaltete Zeitleiste diente im Anschluss an das Jubiläumsevent als Wanderausstellung und wurde in verschiedenen Niederlassungen ausgestellt.

EINE REISE DURCH VERGANGENHEIT, GEGENWART UND ZUKUNFT ALS RÄUMLICH-DRAMATURGISCHES EREIGNIS.

The first space served as a meeting and greeting area and as a dramaturgical introduction. The most important archived milestones and anecdotes of ME Elecmetal were presented by means of a large-scale timeline, like those we are familiar with from museums. The following room extended the timeline with a 360° projection, showing the most important facts surrounding the developed innovations and new technologies. After speeches by the hosts, a projected video reinforced the significance and responsibility emerging from the 100-year existence of the company. The third space, which symbolised the future challenges musically, remained concealed until the end. A fusion of classical instruments and contemporary electronic sounds represented the past, present and future as a coherent entity – and formed the dramatic highlight of the event. The timeline designed for the entrance area served as a touring exhibition after the anniversary event and was exhibited in various locations.

MQ! THE MOBILITY QUOTIENT
PLANWERKSTATT GMBH, BEDBURG-HAU; PLANWORX GMBH, MUNICH; PURE PERFECTION GMBH, WIESBADEN; TISCH13 GMBH, MUNICH

Location
Güterverkehrszentrum Halle B, Ingolstadt

Client
AUDI AG, Ingolstadt

Month / Year
September 2017

Duration
2 days

Dramaturgy / Direction / Coordination
planworx GmbH, Munich

Architecture / Design / Lighting
Planwerkstatt GmbH, Bedburg-Hau

Graphics / Media / Films / Music
tisch13 GmbH, Munich

Artists / Show acts / Decoration
AUDI AG; planworx GmbH

Guest Management / Overall project management
Pure Perfection GmbH, Wiesbaden

Catering
AUDI AG

Realisation
E.W.enture GmbH, Munich

Others
Veranstaltungstechnik ShowEm GmbH, Ingolstadt

Photos
Heinrich Hülser for AUDI AG, Ingolstadt

EIN VIELSEITIGES, THEMENSPEZIFISCHES RAUMDESIGN ALS UNTERSTÜTZENDE KRAFT FÜR NEUE IDEEN UND DENKWEISEN.

Neue Ideen und Innovationen sind das Gold des heutigen Zeitalters. Nicht überraschend, dass viele Events ihre Teilnehmer inspirieren und zu innovativem Denken anregen sollen. So auch der Innovationssummit „MQ! The Mobility Quotient" der AUDI AG. 400 Fachexperten aus allen Bereichen des Lebens wurden nach Ingolstadt geladen, wo der von Pure Perfection, tisch13, planworx und Planwerkstatt gestaltete Summit aktuelle Fragestellungen zum Thema Mobilität vorantreiben sollte. Die Teilnehmer erwartete eine vielseitige Veranstaltung mit zehn Keynote-Speakern, darunter Apple-Mitbegründer Steve Wozniak, und verschiedenen Workshops. Visionen zu Fragestellungen wie „How does smart data make my day" wurden mal mithilfe von Legosteinen, mal mit VR-Brillen und virtuellen Welten bearbeitet.

New ideas and innovations are the gold of the current age. It is not surprising that many events are designed to inspire their participants and stimulate innovative thinking. This was also the case for the innovation summit "MQ! The Mobility Quotient" held by AUDI AG. 400 specialist experts from all walks of life were invited to Ingolstadt, where the summit designed by Pure Perfection, tisch13, planworx and Plan-Werkstatt set out to drive current questions on the topic of mobility forwards. A multifaceted event awaited the participants, with ten keynote speakers including the co-founder of Apple Steve Wozniak and various workshops. Visions surrounding questions such as "How does smart data make my day" were presented with the help of Lego bricks, sometimes with VR glasses and virtual worlds.

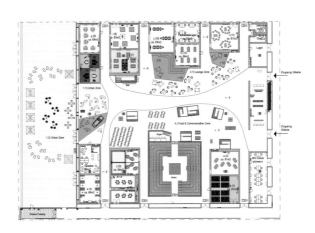

A moiré pattern served as a structuring design element, staging the topic of mobility in its four dimensions – spatial, social, temporal and sustainable. All twelve workshop rooms were individually designed and took up the respective themes for example through floor graphics. At the same time, the spatial event design was intended to activate and inspire. More than a thousand pieces of furniture – from beach loungers, seating cubes and lounge armchairs to bar tables and table football – were available to the guests. The brainstorming for the MQ! formula was recorded in a deliberately traditional manner with chalk on a large board. The link to the digital outside world and the people who were not on site was established by means of a social wall.

A VARIED, THEME-SPECIFIC SPATIAL DESIGN AS A SUPPORTING TOOL FOR NEW IDEAS AND WAYS OF THINKING.

Ein Moiré-Muster diente als gestaltendes Designelement und inszenierte das Thema Mobilität in seinen vier Dimensionen – räumlich, sozial, zeitlich und nachhaltig. Alle zwölf Workshopräume waren individuell gestaltet und griffen die jeweiligen Themen beispielsweise über eine Bodengrafik auf. Gleichzeitig sollte das räumliche Eventdesign aktivieren und inspirieren. So standen den Gästen mehr als tausend unterschiedliche Möbelstücke – von Strandliegen, Sitzwürfeln über Loungesessel bis hin zu Steh- und Kickertischen – zur Verfügung. Die Ideensammlung für die MQ!-Formel wurde bewusst klassisch mit Kreide auf einer großen Tafel festgehalten. Die Verbindung zur digitalen Außenwelt und den Menschen, die nicht vor Ort waren, wurde über eine Social Wall geschaffen.

„SMART GERMANY" –
DEUTSCHER INGENIEURTAG DES VDI
PASSEPARTOUT – AGENTUR FÜR EVENTS GMBH, MEERBUSCH

Location
Maritim Hotel, Dusseldorf

Client
VDI Verein Deutscher Ingenieure e.V., Dusseldorf

Month / Year
May 2017

Duration
1 day

Dramaturgy / Direction / Coordination
Passepartout – Agentur für Events GmbH, Meerbusch

Lighting / Media / Realisation
Aventem GmbH, Hilden

Films
BECKDESIGN GmbH, Bochum

Artists / Show acts
Fantastic Five, Cologne; Sven West / Westbunch, Grevenbroich

Catering
Maritim Hotel, Dusseldorf

Photos
VDI Verein Deutscher Ingenieure e.V., Dusseldorf

FLEXIBLE BÜHNEN-ELEMENTE INSZE-NIEREN DAS JAHRES-THEMA SOWIE DEN MENSCHEN ALS IMPULSGEBER FÜR WANDEL UND BEWEGUNG.

Die Digitalisierung der Arbeitswelt war nicht nur das VDI-Jahresthema 2017, sondern gleichzeitig auch das Motto des 28. Deutschen Ingenieurstages. Im Mai 2017 lud der VDI (Verein Deutscher Ingenieure) rund 1.400 Gäste aus Politik, Wirtschaft, Verbänden und Hochschulen ein, um sich der Zukunft von Arbeit im Kontext digitaler Transformation zu widmen. Die Aufgabe der betreuenden Agentur Passepartout war es, bestehende Veranstaltungs-elemente in ein neues Raum- und Bühnenkonzept zu integrieren und das Jahresthema im Eventdesign aufzugreifen.

The digitisation of the world of work was not only the VDI theme of the year 2017, but also the motto of the 28th German Engineer Day. In May 2017, VDI (Verein Deutscher Ingenieure/Association of German Engineers) invited around 1,400 guests from politics, economics, associations and universities to focus on the future of work in the context of digital transformation. The task for the responsible agency Passepartout was to integrate existing event elements into a new spatial and stage concept and to take up the theme of the year in the event design.

Wandel wurde nicht nur inhaltlich, sondern auch im Bühnenkonzept zum zentralen Thema. Flexible, unterschiedlich große Bühnenwände konnten auf verschiedenen Ebenen bespielt und immer wieder neu platziert werden. Über den Nachmittag und Abend hinweg entstanden immer wieder neue Settings. Die Positionswechsel wurden tänzerisch inszeniert und symbolisierten den Menschen als Impulsgeber, der den Wandel in Bewegung bringt. Mit der so gewonnenen Wandlungsfähigkeit der Bühne konnten die Protagonisten sowie das Programm unterschiedlich in Szene gesetzt werden. Das fünfstündige Bühnenprogramm beinhaltete Podiumsdiskussionen, Performances, Vorträge sowie die Ehrung von Jungingenieuren und Mitgliedern, die sich um den VDI verdient gemacht haben. Die gesamte Veranstaltung wurde live gestreamt, Highlights in Echtzeit bei Facebook veröffentlicht und die Grundsatzrede des Präsidenten im Anschluss bei YouTube hochgeladen. Der VDI-Blog informierte parallel zu der Veranstaltung über die Geschehnisse vor Ort.

FLEXIBLE STAGE ELEMENTS PRESENT THE THEME OF THE YEAR, AS WELL AS MAN AS AN INSTIGATOR OF CHANGE AND MOTION.

Change was a central theme not only of the content, but also of the stage concept. Flexible stage walls of different sizes could be animated on different levels and be continuously repositioned. Over the course of the afternoon and evening, a whole series of new settings was created. The changes in position were staged with dance and symbolised man as an instigator, providing impulses and setting change into motion. Owing to the versatility of the setting, it was possible to stage the protagonists and the programme variously. The five-hour stage programme contained podium discussions, performances, presentations and the honouring of young engineers and members worthy of the VDI. The whole event was streamed live, highlights were published in real time on Facebook and the keynote speech by the president was then uploaded onto YouTube. The VDI blog provided information about events as they unfolded, alongside the event.

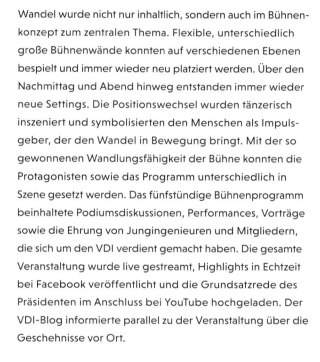

MIELE LAUNCH EVENT
DREINULL AGENTUR FÜR MEDIATAINMENT GMBH & CO. KG, BERLIN

Location
BOLLE Festsäle, Berlin

Client
Miele Hausgeräte International, Gütersloh

Month / Year
August 2017

Duration
several days

Dramaturgy / Direction/ Coordination / Architecture / Design / Graphics
DREINULL Agentur für Mediatainment GmbH & Co. KG, Berlin; MetaDesign GmbH, Berlin

Lighting / Media
AMBION GmbH, Berlin

Films
DNM | DREINULLMOTION GmbH, Berlin

Music
Looptrigger, Berlin; Julian Laping, Berlin

Artists / Show acts
battleROYAL GmbH, Berlin

Decoration
Raumsektor GBR, Berlin; WERKSTOFF, Berlin

Catering
Markus Herbicht Catering, Berlin; in collaboration with Miele Dialog oven chefs

Others
trommsdorff + drüner, A Reply AG Company, Berlin (Data-driven marketing); DELASOCIAL GmbH, Hamburg (Digital communication)

Photos
Markus Adamovský, Prague

Viele Marketingevents nutzen große dramaturgische Effekte, um Produktneuheiten vorzustellen. Im Rahmen der Auftaktveranstaltung zur Markteinführung des Miele Dialoggarers wählte DREINULL weitere Stilmittel, um der innovativen Technologie des Geräts gerecht zu werden. Ein direktes Erleben sollte das Innovationspotenzial dieser neuen Gerätegattung verdeutlichen. Anlässlich der weltweiten Markteinführung lud Miele ausgewählte Gäste zu einer von acht Veranstaltungen an vier Tagen ein. Ein bewusst klassisch gehaltener Stehempfang mit Podiumsbeiträgen rund um das Thema „Mieles Tradition der Innovation" schuf zu Beginn einer jeden Veranstaltung den Eindruck, einem eher traditionellen Event beizuwohnen – bis sich schließlich in einem unerwarteten Moment ein medial bespielter Tunnel öffnete, durch den die Gäste in den eigentlichen Veranstaltungsbereich geleitet wurden.

Many marketing events make use of great dramaturgical effects to introduce new products. In the context of the kick-off event for the market launch of the Miele 'Dialog oven', DREINULL chose additional stylistic means to reflect the innovative technology of the appliance. Direct experiences were designed to show the innovation potential of this new type of appliance. On the occasion of the worldwide market launch, Miele invited selected guests to one of eight events on four days. A deliberately conventional standing reception at the beginning of each event with speeches from a rostrum on the topic of "Miele's tradition of innovation" created the impression of attending a rather traditional event – until, as an unexpected moment, a tunnel with media animation opened up, through which the guests were led into the actual event area.

Eingebettet in eine großformatige Medieninstallation auf Wänden und Tischen enthüllte sich ein weitläufiger Gastraum mit sechs großen Tischen und Dialoggarer-Stationen. Die Gäste wurden nun von Köchen direkt an den Tischen unter dem Motto „Revolutionary excellence" durch ein Menü geleitet, das mit konventionellen Kochmethoden nicht herzustellen gewesen wäre. Über den Lachs, der in einem Stück – zum Teil gegart, zum Teil als Ceviche – serviert wurde, oder mittels des Signature Dishes, eines Kabeljaus, der in einer Eisbox zubereitet wurde, ohne dass diese schmilzt: Dem Dialoggarer wurde eine ideale Bühne geschaffen, um die Gäste unmittelbar zu beeindrucken.

EIN ÜBERRASCHENDES PRODUKT PRÄSENTIERT SICH MIT EINEM DRAMATURGISCH EBENSO ÜBERRASCHENDEN EVENT.

A SURPRISING PRODUCT IS PRESENTED THROUGH AN EVENT WITH AN EQUALLY SURPRISING DRAMATURGY.

Surrounded by a large-format media installation on walls and tables, an extensive guest room was revealed with six big tables and 'Dialog oven' stations. Guided by chefs directly at their tables, the guests were then led through a menu that could not have been made using conventional cooking methods, true to the motto "Revolutionary excellence". Whether it was the salmon that was served whole – partly cooked, partly as ceviche – or the signature dish, a cod fish prepared in an ice box that stayed frozen, an ideal stage was created for the 'Dialog oven' to impress the guests directly.

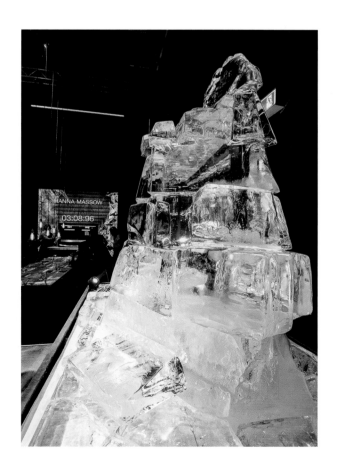

HALL OF FAME
DER DEUTSCHEN FORSCHUNG
JAZZUNIQUE GMBH, FRANKFURT A. MAIN

Location
Palmengarten, Frankfurt a. Main

Client
Merck KGaA, Darmstadt

Month / Year
November 2017

Duration
1 day

Dramaturgy / Architecture / Design / Graphics
Jazzunique GmbH, Frankfurt a. Main

Direction / Coordination
Andreana Clemenz / PIO Entertainment, Wiesbaden

Media / Realisation
D4MANCE, Viernheim

Music
Songs & Signals, Wiesbaden

Catering
Restaurant Lafleur, Frankfurt a. Main; Hubertus Tzschirner, Bad Nauheim

Photos
Kristof Lemp Fotografie, Darmstadt

Die „Hall of Fame der deutschen Forschung" zeichnet alljährlich außergewöhnliche Forscher und Unternehmen aus, die sich durch bahnbrechende Ideen in der deutschen Forschungslandschaft hervorgetan haben. Gastgeber sind das Wissenschafts- und Technologieunternehmen Merck und das *manager magazin*. Im konzeptionellen Fokus der Abendveranstaltung und Awardverleihung im Jahr 2017 standen „Die Facetten des Gelingens". Jazzunique thematisierte die Persönlichkeitsfacetten der Menschen, die darauf brennen, Neues zu entdecken und Innovationen zu entwickeln. Eigenschaften wie Offenheit, Kreativität, Ausdauer, Mut und Vertrauen sollten in einer audiovisuellen Inszenierung zum Ausdruck gebracht werden.

The "Hall of Fame of German Research" presents awards every year to exceptional researchers and companies that have distinguished themselves in the German research world through groundbreaking ideas. The hosts are the science and technology company Merck and *manager magazine*. The conceptual focus of the evening event and award ceremony in 2017 was on "The Facets of Success". Jazzunique thematised the personality attributes of the people who are driven to discover something new and develop innovations. Traits such as openness, creativity, perseverance, courage and faith were expressed in an audiovisual presentation.

PERSÖNLICHKEITS-FACETTEN SYMBOLISIERT UND INSZENIERT MITHILFE KINETISCHER LICHT-OBJEKTE UND INSTRUMENTE.

An der Decke des Saals und über den Köpfen der Gäste schwebten „Kinetic Lights", die immer wieder neue Raumstrukturen formten. Abgestimmt auf den inszenatorischen Moment symbolisierten die bewegten Lichtobjekte mal „wilde Kreativität", mal „wellenförmige Ausdauer". Akustisches Ausdrucksmittel waren Instrumente, die den Persönlichkeitsfacetten zugeordnet wurden. In einzelnen Akten sollten Piano, Geige, Cello und Saxofon die Attribute musikalisch wiedergeben und zum Abschluss ein harmonisches Ensemble bilden. Jazzunique zeichnete sich auch für die Gestaltung des Awards verantwortlich, der durch seine Maserung die Etappen der individuellen Schaffensgeschichte der Forscher abbildete.

"Kinetic lights", forming continually changing spatial structures, floated on the ceiling of the hall and over the heads of the guests. The moving light objects, attuned to the staged moment, sometimes symbolised "wild creativity" and sometimes "undulating endurance". Instruments assigned to the personality facets provided an acoustic means of expression. The piano, violin, cello and saxophone represented the attributes musically in individual acts, forming a harmonious ensemble as the finale. Jazzunique was responsible for the design of the awards, whose surface depicted the stages in the individual achievement history of the researchers.

PERSONALITY TRAITS ARE SYMBOLISED AND PRESENTED BY MEANS OF KINETIC LIGHT OBJECTS AND INSTRUMENTS.

LAUNCH-EVENT NEXT47 „OPEN UP!"
HW.DESIGN GMBH, MUNICH

Location
Kesselhaus, Munich

Client
next47 GmbH, Munich

Month / Year
December 2016

Duration
1 day

Dramaturgy / Direction / Coordination / Architecture / Design / Graphics
hw.design gmbh, Munich

Media
WBLT Veranstaltungstechnik GmbH & Co. KG, Oberhausen

Decoration
AKBevent GmbH & Co. KG, Martinsried

Catering
FR Event- und MesseCatering GmbH, Eibelstadt

Realisation
AKBevent GmbH & Co. KG; Projektstark GmbH & Co. KG, Unterhaching

Photos
Willi Nothers, Dusseldorf

Das von Siemens neu gegründete Unternehmen next47 möchte Start-ups finanziell sowie mit Erfahrung und Know-how unterstützen. Um die neue Firma, ihre Vision und Strategie der Start-up-Community sowie der Presse vorzustellen, konzipierte und realisierte hw.design im Dezember 2016 ein aktivierendes Launch-Event. Mehr als 300 Gäste aus dem In- und Ausland, namhafte Redner und Start-ups waren geladen. Integraler Bestandteil des Eventdesigns war das Motto „Open up!". Verschiedene interaktive Elemente luden die Gäste zur aktiven Teilnahme ein: Durchgänge in mobilen Zwischenwänden sollten symbolische Türen öffnen und Grenzen überschreiten; Sitzhocker, die die Teilnehmer schnell und einfach selbst aufbauen konnten, vermittelten eine Hands-on-Mentalität.

The company next47 newly founded by Siemens seeks to support start-ups both financially and with experience and expertise. To present the new company, its vision and strategy to the start-up community and the press, hw.design designed and realised a dynamic launch event in December 2016. More than 300 guests from home and abroad, renowned speakers and start-ups were invited. An integral component of the event design was the motto "Open up!". Various interactive elements invited guests to participate actively: passageways through mobile partition walls were designed to open symbolic doors and step beyond boundaries. Stools that the participants could assemble quickly and easily themselves conveyed a hands-on mentality.

AKTIVIERENDE EVENTDESIGN-ELEMENTE MACHEN DAS MOTTO „OPEN UP!" UND EINE HANDS-ON-MENTALITÄT GREIFBAR.

DYNAMIC EVENT DESIGN ELEMENTS CONVEY THE MOTTO "OPEN UP!" AND A HANDS-ON MENTALITY.

Zum Ende der Veranstaltung öffnete sich die Bühnenrückwand und gab einen weiteren Raum frei. Dort präsentierten ausgewählte Start-ups ihre Ideen und Produkte und standen für einen Austausch zur Verfügung. Eine anschließende Open Bar mit Open Dinner sollte einen flexiblen und authentischen Charakter kommunizieren und ein lockeres Get-together unter den Gästen fördern. Die Veranstaltung war der Start einer Eventreihe, die an den internationalen Standorten von next47 im Jahr 2017 stattfand. Eine Website und Social-Media-Präsenzen begleiteten die Events und gaben Einblicke in aktuelle Aktivitäten des neuen Unternehmens.

At the end of the event, the rear wall of the stage opened and revealed a further space where selected start-ups presented their ideas and products and were available for exchanges. An adjoining Open Bar with an Open Dinner was intended to communicate a flexible and authentic character and to encourage a casual get-together among the guests. The event was the start of a series of events that took place in 2017 at the international locations of next47. A website and social media presences accompanied the events and provided insights into the new company's current activities.

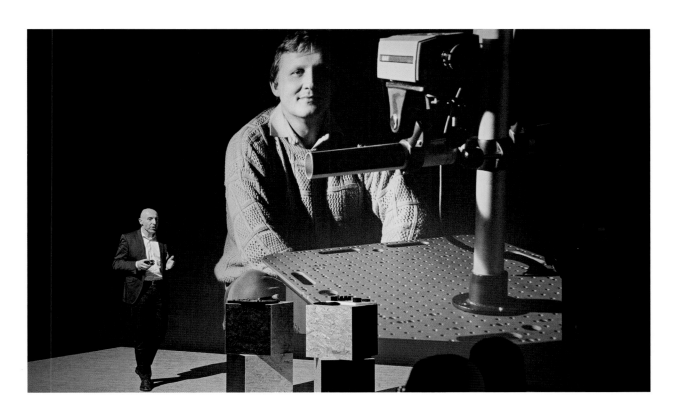

YOUTUBE FESTIVAL
INSGLÜCK GESELLSCHAFT FÜR MARKENINSZENIERUNG MBH, BERLIN

Location
Heizkraftwerk Berlin-Mitte, Berlin

Client
Google Deutschland GmbH, Berlin

Month / Year
September 2016

Duration
1 day

Dramaturgy
insglück Gesellschaft für Markeninszenierung mbH, Berlin

Direction / Coordination
Harry Seedorf, Berlin

Architecture / Design
Markus Wagner / insglück; Jan Pfeuffer, Berlin; Altspace, Berlin; Dimitar Nikolaev, Berlin; Rico Dietzel, Berlin

Graphics
Katharina Ploog, Berlin; Silke Roßbach, Berlin

Lighting
Henning Schletter / imaginary lights, Fehrbellin

Media
B-Reel, Berlin

Films
B-Reel; Mainpicture, Hamburg

Artists / Show acts
My Virgin Kitchen / Barry Lewis, Weston-super-Mare (Food-Channel); CookBakery / Duygu, Friedberg (Food-Channel); Marquese Scott, Lawrenceville (Popping dancer); freekickerz / Athletia, Cologne (Parcour performance breakdance, Free-Running, Basketball, Fußball-Freestyle); Duke, Cheltenham (Beatboxing); Alle Farben, Berlin (DJ / Musician)

Decoration
BALLONI GmbH, Cologne

Catering
Bite Club, Berlin

Realisation
Nüssli, Ludwigsfelde

Photos
Markus Mielek, Dortmund; Stefan Hoederath, Berlin; YouTube, Berlin

Google veranstaltet bereits seit einigen Jahren eine Kreativ- und Leistungsshow in Form eines Events. Im Jahr 2016 sollte insglück ein neues Format entwickeln, das den Fokus ausschließlich auf das wichtigste Medium YouTube legt. Um die Marketingmöglichkeiten aufzuzeigen und den Spirit der Marke zu transportieren, wurde aus der vorherigen Marketingkonferenz ein Festival. Ziel war es, die vielfältige Welt von YouTube vom Screen ins wahre Leben zu holen. Sowohl die Location, das Berliner Kraftwerk, als auch das Eventdesign, bestehend aus kräftigen Farben, Projektionen auf Steinwänden und Graffitis, sollten den Spirit der Marke auf den ersten Blick spürbar machen.

Google has been holding a creative and performance show for several years now in the form of an event. In 2016, insglück was to develop a new format that placed the focus exclusively on the most important medium YouTube. To convey the marketing possibilities and the spirit of the brand, the previous marketing conference became a festival. The goal was to bring the colourful world of YouTube from the screen into real life. Both the location – the Berlin power plant – and the event design consisting of vibrant colours, projections on stone walls and graffiti were designed to make the spirit of the brand evident at first glance.

**EINE MARKETING-
KONFERENZ, DIE
KEINE IST – SONDERN
EIN FESTIVAL. INFOR-
MATIV, INTERAKTIV
UND MIT HOHEM
UNTERHALTUNGSWERT.**

Verschiedene Bereiche und Demo-Stationen luden zum Ausprobieren neuester Technologien, wie 360°- und VR-Video-Produktion, ein. Großzügige Lounges schufen Raum für Networking. Spielerische Elemente, wie das YouTube-Quiz oder der Freezeframe-Fotostand, boten einen hohen Unterhaltungswert und eine Abwechslung zu fachlichen Informationen. Inhalte zu Werbemöglichkeiten und Strategien auf YouTube wurden in zwölf Masterclasses vermittelt. Auf der Festival-Hauptbühne fanden Opening und Finale mit Key Notes und Live-Performances statt. Auch das Catering war integraler Bestandteil des Konzepts: eine Mischung aus Berliner Street-Food und Spezialitäten von YouTubern mit erfolgreichen Kochkanälen. Entsprechend der Zielgruppe erfolgte die gesamte Kommunikation mit den Gästen digital. Eine eigene Website bündelte Informationen zum Programm, ermöglichte die Abstimmung über die Themen der zwölf Masterclasses sowie die spätere Registrierung. Das Follow-up bestand aus einem Feedback-Newsletter und einem Think-With-Google-Channel.

Various areas and demo stations invited visitors to try out the latest technologies, such as 360° and VR video production. Generous lounges provided networking forums. Playful elements, such as the YouTube quiz or the freeze frame photo stand, offered a high entertainment value and a change from objective information. Content about advertising opportunities and strategies on YouTube was conveyed in twelve masterclasses. The opening and finale with key notes and live performances took place on the main festival stage. The catering was also an integral part of the concept: a mixture of Berlin street food and specialities by YouTubers with successful cooking channels. In line with the target group, the entire guest communication was digital. A designated website gathered information about the programme, allowed votes on the topics of the twelve masterclasses, as well as registration afterwards. The follow-up consisted of a feedback newsletter and a Think with Google channel.

A MARKETING CONFERENCE THAT IS NOT A CONFERENCE BUT A FESTIVAL. INFORMATIVE, INTERACTIVE AND WITH A HIGH ENTERTAINMENT VALUE.

VIESSMANN AR PRESENTATION
ATELIER MARKGRAPH GMBH, FRANKFURT A. MAIN

Location
Messe Frankfurt, Frankfurt a. Main

Client
*Viessmann Werke GmbH & Co. KG,
Allendorf (Eder)*

Month / Year
March 2017

Duration
several days

Architecture / Design
Atelier Markgraph GmbH, Frankfurt a. Main

Graphic Production
Leko Grafische Produktionen, Weinstadt

Lighting
Neumann&Müller Gmbh & Co. KG, Ratingen

Media
*NSYNK Gesellschaft für Kunst und Technik
mbH, Frankfurt a. Main / Berlin;
Neumann&Müller GmbH & Co. KG*

Films
*Acht Frankfurt GmbH, Frankfurt a. Main
(Motion design, Post production)*

Photos
Kristof Lemp, Darmstadt

DIGITALISIERUNG ANSCHAULICH ERKLÄRT – MITHILFE VON AUGMENTED REALITY UND INTEN-SIVEM AUSTAUSCH.

Die Digitalisierung sorgt für Veränderungen und Umwäl-zungen in allen Branchen. Trotzdem haben viele Menschen Hemmungen, Themen wie „Customer Centricity" oder „Design Thinking" anzugehen und in ihrem Berufsalltag zu integrieren – eine Problematik, der Viessmann mit seiner Zielgruppe aus Monteuren und Heizungsfachleuten häufig begegnet. Aus diesem Grund sollten auf der ISH 2017 (Messe für den Verbund aus Wasser und Energie) das Thema Digitalisierung aus der Perspektive des Handwerks aufgear-beitet und Chancen nachvollziehbar kommuniziert werden. Fünf von Atelier Markgraph entwickelte mediale Pfeilstationen durchliefen alltägliche Arbeitsschritte und veranschaulichten, wie digitale Tools die Projektprozesse unterstützen.

Digitisation is bringing about changes and revolutions in all sectors. Even so, many people are reluctant to tackle topics such as "customer centricity" of "design thinking" and to in-tegrate them into everyday working life. This is an issue that Viessmann encounters often with its target group of installers and heating specialists. For this reason, at ISH 2017 (trade fair for the water and energy sectors) the topic of digitisation was to be presented from the perspective of installation trades, with a clear communication of its potential. Five arrow-shaped media stations developed by Atelier Markgraph ran through everyday working steps and showed how digital tools support various project processes.

DIGITISATION EXPLAINED CLEARLY – WITH THE HELP OF AUGMENTED REALITY AND LIVELY EXCHANGES.

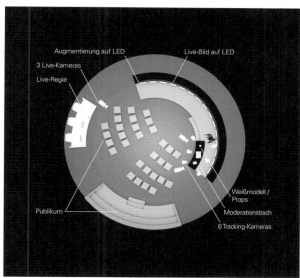

Im zentralen Forum des Stands machten Viessmann-Experten in zehnminütigen Augmented-Reality-Präsentationen live und in Echtzeit die vielfältigen Möglichkeiten, die sich aus der Vernetzung von Haus, Heizung und Handwerkersoftware ergeben, fassbar. Augmented Reality wurde dabei zu einem intelligenten didaktischen Tool, das digitale – also physisch nicht sichtbare – Abläufe sichtbar machte. Dafür wurden reale Objekte und Weißmodelle von Kameras getrackt, auf einer Medienfläche durch Text und Grafik ergänzt, und so informativ eingebettet. An den fünf Messetagen fanden 190 Augmented-Reality-Shows statt. Im Halbstundentakt präsentierten insgesamt acht Experten die Chancen der Digitalsierung für neue digitale Geschäftsmodelle, für vereinfachte Prozesse und nicht zuletzt für die Energiewende. So bot das Forum nicht nur einen Rahmen für Informationsvermittlung, sondern ebenso für intensiven Gedankenaustausch und die gemeinsame Entwicklung von Lösungen.

In the central forum of the stand, Viessmann experts made the many possibilities emerging from the networking of house, heating and technical software tangible through ten-minute augmented reality presentations, live and in real time. Augmented reality thereby became an intelligent didactic tool that made digital – i.e. physically not visible – processes visible. Real objects and white models White models were tracked by cameras, supplemented with text and graphics on a media surface, with an informative aspect. 190 augmented reality shows took place on the five exhibition days. Every half an hour, a total of eight experts presented the opportunities opened up by digitisation for new digital business models, simplified processes and not least for the energy revolution. The forum offered a framework not only for conveying information, but also for a lively exchange of ideas and the joint development of solutions.

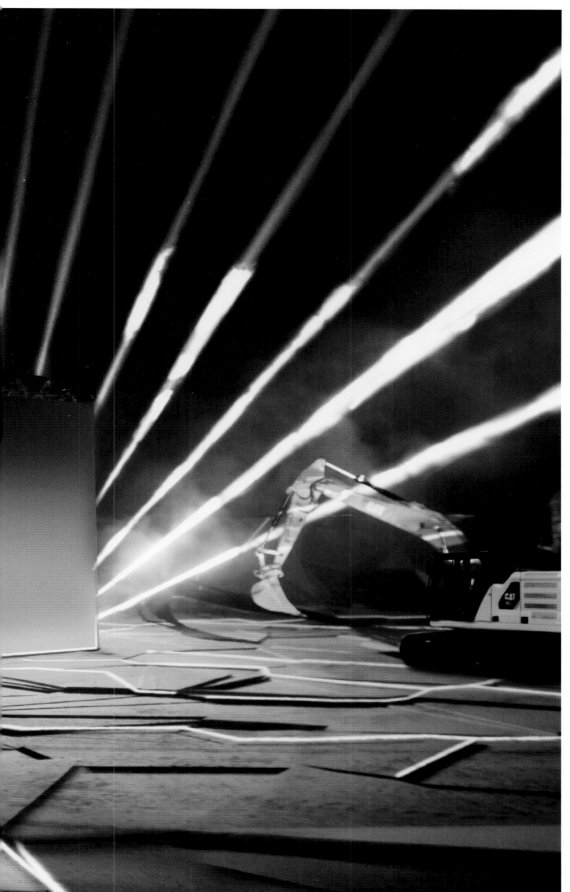

CATERPILLAR CHALLENGER DAYS
TISCH13 GMBH, MUNICH

Location
Caterpillar Demonstration and Learning Center, Málaga

Client
Caterpillar Construction Europe, Middle East & Africa, Geneva

Month / Year
September – October 2017

Duration
several days

Dramaturgy / Direction / Coordination / Architecture / Design / Graphics
tisch13 GmbH, Munich

Lighting
intermediate Engineering GmbH, Hamburg

Media / Films
Urbanscreen GmbH & Co. KG, Bremen

Music
Urbanscreen GmbH & Co. KG, Bremen; André Feldhaus, Bremen; Anders Wasserfall, Bremen / Oslo

Realisation
PRG Deutschland, Hamburg

Photos
Ernesto Oehler, Málaga

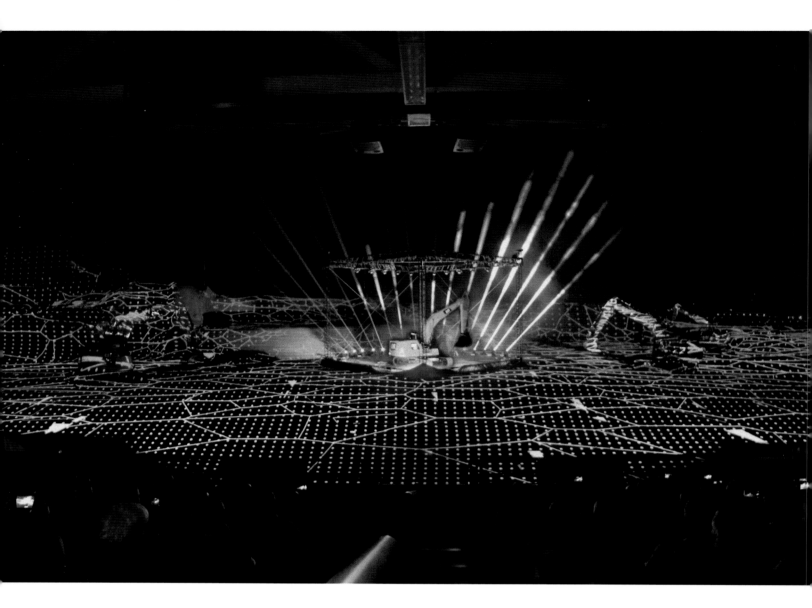

Die neue Produktgeneration des Baggerherstellers Caterpillar stellte vor dem Hintergrund der digitalen Transformation einen tiefgreifenden Wandel der Produktstrategie dar. Entsprechend spektakulär und aufsehenerregend sollte die Weltpremiere werden, zu der 1.500 Zuschauer an sechs Abenden geladen waren. Unter dem Titel „Night of the Challenger" inszenierte tisch13 die neuen Produkte in ihrem „natürlichen" Umfeld: einem überdimensionalen „Outdoor-Sandkasten" im Caterpillar Trainingscenter in Malaga.

The new product generation made by the digger manufacturer Caterpillar represented a fundamental change in product strategy in the light of digital transformation. The world premiere, to which 1,500 spectators were invited on six evenings, was therefore designed to be spectacular and sensational. Under the title "Night of the Challenger", tisch13 staged the new product generation in its "natural" surroundings: an oversized "outdoor sandpit" at the Caterpillar training centre in Malaga.

EINE SPEKTAKULÄRE, ÜBERDIMENSIONALE OPEN-AIR-PERFORMANCE FÜR EIN ENTSPRECHEND IMPOSANTES PRODUKT.

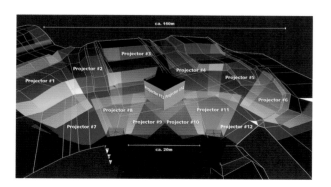

Die Open-Air-Performance bespielte eine Fläche von über 4.500 Quadratmetern auf einer Gesamtfläche von 100 Metern Breite und 45 Metern Tiefe mit Projection Mapping. 14 Hochleistungsprojektoren mit einer Gesamtleistung von über 280.000 ANSI-Lumen sorgten für eine beeindruckende und flächendeckende Bespielung der Outdoor-Arena in einer hochauflösenden 5K-Medienproduktion. Ein im Zentrum stehender Kubus diente als zusätzliche Projektionsfläche und zur anfänglichen Verhüllung des neuen Produkts. Mithilfe eines doppelten Kabuki-Fallvorhangs wurde die Produktenthüllung in zwei markanten Highlights inszeniert. Die 16-minütige Show war in drei theatergleiche Akte unterteilt und führte inhaltlich durch die Anfänge des Unternehmens im 20. Jahrhundert bis zu den aktuellen Herausforderungen im digitalen Zeitalter. Um die Weltpremiere und die neuen Caterpillar-Produkte spürbar vom bestehenden Corporate Design abzuheben, wurden das Motion- und Sounddesign sowie die gesamte grafische Bespielung speziell für dieses Ereignis neu konzipiert und komponiert.

The open-air performance animated an area of over 4,500 square metres, measuring 100 metres wide and 45 metres deep, with projection mapping. 14 high-performance projectors with a total strength of 280,000 ANSI lumen provided an impressive and extensive animation of the outdoor arena with a high-resolution 5K media production. A cube at the centre served as an additional projection surface and as an initial concealment of the new product. The product revelation was presented as two striking highlights, with the help of a double Kabuki dropping curtain. The 16-minute show was divided into three equal acts whose content led from the beginnings of the company in the 20th century through to the current challenges in the digital age. To make the world premiere and the new Caterpillar products stand out distinctly from the existing corporate design, the motion and sound design, as well as the entire graphic animation, were newly conceived and composed especially for this event.

A SPECTACULAR, LARGE-SCALE OPEN-AIR PERFORMANCE FOR AN EQUALLY IMPRESSIVE PRODUCT.

Jan Kalbfleisch, sind Events als einzelne Marketingmaßnahme noch klar abgrenzbar? Lässt sich nach wie vor eine Grenze zu Messeerlebnissen oder Raumerfahrungen ziehen? Schaut man sich im diesjährigen Eventdesign Jahrbuch um, deuten auffällig viele Projekte darauf hin, dass es diese klaren Grenzen nicht mehr gibt. Kategorisierungen nach bislang bestehenden Kriterien waren in dieser Ausgabe besonders schwierig. Doch ist diese Beobachtung tatsächlich ein übergreifender Trend? Zeigt sich diese Entwicklung womöglich auch in anderen Bereichen, Chancen oder Herausforderungen?

Ich beobachte diese Entwicklung gleichermaßen. Jedoch längst nicht nur auf Ebene der Projekte. Auch die Unternehmen unserer Branche erscheinen zunehmend unscharf an den Leistungsrändern. Mir wäre nicht ein Unternehmen ab einer gewissen Größe bekannt, das nicht digital ebenso macht, wie live ... und Messe ... und Event ... und PR ... und wenn erforderlich, alles zusammen. Dabei verbietet sich jedoch der naheliegende „Hans Dampf in allen Gassen"-Vorwurf. Denn die Erbringung dieser Leistungen erfolgt meistens in fein ziselierten und jahrelang erprobten Netzwerken aus Spezialisten unterschiedlichster Herkunft und Größe.

Warum sie das machen? Weil es die Kunden fordern! Die Leistungen unserer Branche waren bis vor wenigen Jahren meist singuläre Kommunikationsinstrumente unserer Kunden mit ihren Stakeholdern – egal ob Messe oder Event, ob Kunden oder Mitarbeiter. Es waren in sich geschlossene und sauber abgegrenzte Ereignisse. Dies hat sich erheblich verändert. In zunehmendem Maße erkennen die Kunden den großen Nutzen der Live-Kommunikation und damit die herausragende Bedeutung im unternehmerischen Kommunikationsmix.

STATT EINER SITUATIVEN BETRACHTUNG WIRD LIVE-KOMMUNIKATION MEHR UND MEHR PROZESSUAL UND PERMANENT GEDACHT.

Damit einhergeht geht natürlich eine immer stärkere Verschränkung mit anderen Formaten, Kanälen, Medien. Und damit einhergeht eben auch eine wachsende Unschärfe hinsichtlich unserer klassischen Kategorisierung.

Dies jedoch scheint mir, wenn überhaupt, ein kleiner Preis. Denn die Chancen für Live steigen damit erheblich. Das Risiko liegt wohl darin, in der zunehmenden Fokussierung auf Strategie nicht zu verlieren, was unsere Branche bisher ausgezeichnet hat: große Kreativität, Spontaneität, Experimentierfreude und letztlich operative Exzellenz. Doch da vertraue ich uns schon sehr – denn ganz zu „bändigen" sein werden wir wohl nie.

Als Geschäftsführer des FAMAB Kommunikationsverband e.V. sei mir abschließend erlaubt, zu bemerken, dass wir diese Entwicklung antizipiert haben und seit über fünf Jahren keine Kategorisierung der Mitgliedsunternehmen mehr haben. Und um den Kritikern ihre Chance zu nehmen: Ja, bei unseren Awards versuchen wir bis zum heutigen Tage, eingereichte Arbeiten sinnvoll zu kategorisieren. Wir sind eben auch nur „auf dem Weg".

Jan Kalbfleisch studierte Wirtschaftsingenieurwesen und ist Geschäftsführer des FAMAB e.V. Bevor es ihn in die Live-Kommunikation zog, arbeitete er in der Medienbranche als Unternehmensberater und in der Geschäftsleitung von Medienhäusern. Als Geschäftsführer einer Eventagentur realisierte er innovative Vortrags- und Weiterbildungsformate. Nebenberuflich dozierte er an der Hochschule der Medien in Stuttgart.

www.famab.de

WO SIND DENN BLOSS DIE GRENZEN HIN?
WHERE HAVE THE BOUNDARIES GONE?
COMMENTARY BY JAN KALBFLEISCH, FAMAB E.V.

Jan Kalbfleisch, are events still clearly delimitable as individual marketing events? Is it still possible to draw a boundary between events and exhibition experiences or spatial experiences? If one browses through this year's Event Design Yearbook, a conspicuous number of projects indicate that there are no longer any clear boundaries. Categorisations according to previous criteria were especially difficult in this edition. But is this observation really an overall trend? Is this development perhaps also evident in other areas, opportunities or challenges?

I have also been observing this development, but for a long time it has not only been in terms of projects. The companies in our industry are also increasingly blurred at the edges. I do not know any company of a certain size that does not do digital alongside live... and exhibition... and event... and PR... and if necessary all of these together. However, the obvious accusation of "Jack of all trades" is scarcely permissible, as these achievements are usually the result of finely honed networks of specialists from a wide variety of backgrounds who have proven themselves for years.

Why do they do this? Because customers demand it! Until recently, the services of our industry were usually singular communication tools for our customers with their stakeholders – whether it was a trade fair or event, customers or employees. They were self-contained and cleanly defined events. This has changed significantly. Customers are increasingly recognising the great benefit of live communication and therefore its considerable importance in the corporate communication matrix.

And, of course, more and more interweaving with other formats, channels and media goes hand in hand with this. It follows then that there is also a growing lack of clarity regarding our traditional categorisation.

However, this appears to me to be a small price to pay, if at all, because the live opportunities increase significantly as a result. I suppose the risk lies in the increasing focus on strategy and not losing what has hitherto distinguished our industry: great creativity, spontaneity, an experimental attitude and lastly operative excellence. I have faith in us though – as I doubt we will ever be really "tamed".

As Managing Director of FAMAB Kommunikationsverband e.V., let me remark in conclusion that we anticipated this development and have had no categorisation of member companies for more than five years. And to take the wind out of critics' sails: yes, at our awards we try to this very day to classify submitted work meaningfully. We are, after all, just "on the path".

INSTEAD OF A PREDOMINANTLY SITUATIONAL VIEW ON IT, LIVE COMMUNICATION IS INCREASINGLY BEING THOUGHT OF AS A CONTINUOUS PROCESS.

Jan Kalbfleisch studied industrial engineering and is Managing Director of FAMAB e.V. Before he ventured into Live Communication, he worked in the media sector, as a business consultant and in the management of media companies. As the Managing Director of an events agency, he realised innovative presentation and further training formats. Alongside this, he was also a part-time lecturer at the Media University in Stuttgart.

www.famab.de

/\ventem
Audiovisuelle Dienstleistungen

Service

Aventem offers high level technical and constructional planning and implementation of coporate events, fair stands, television shows, and conferences.

In detail we offer media technics and services, illumination, audio, booth construction, rigging icl. Sil3 systems, stage and scenery.

Aventem provides full service, and delivers from its office and warehouse close to Dusseldorf to customers worldwide. With its own wood, electronic, and metal factory, as well as large logistc capacities Aventem offers great flexibility for the realisation of projects.

References

Deutsche Bank AG, Targo Bank, Deutsche Apotheker & Ärzte Bank, Verein Deutscher Ingenieure, MVDA / Linda AG, Allianz AG, ThyssenKrupp AG, Rittal GmbH & Co. KG, Vorwerk Elektrowerke GmbH & Co. KG, Rewe Zentral AG, Bayer AG, Siemens AG, E.ON, Uniper SE, RWE AG, Toyota Deutschland, Honda, Skoda AG, Volkswagen AG, Daimler AG, Falken Tyre Europe GmbH, MAN AG, Rheinmetall AG, Vodafone AG, Huawei Deutschland GmbH, Max Brinkmann KG, Zweites Deutsches Fernsehen, Westdeutscher Rundfunk, SWR, ARD

Contact

Herderstraße 70
40721 Hilden
Germany
Phone: +49 2103 25230-0
www.aventem.de
info@aventem.de

IMPRESSUM
IMPRINT

Author	Katharina Stein
Editing / Setting	Kim Bachmann
Translation	Lynne Kolar-Thompson
Layout	Tina Agard Grafik & Buchdesign, Esslingen / Neckar
Lithography	corinna rieber prepress, Marbach / Neckar
Printing	Gorenjski tisk storitve, Kranj
Paper	Hello Fat Matt 1,1 / 150 g/m^2
Cover photo	Klaus Bossemeyer, Münster, Olympus Perspective Playground by VITAMIN E – Gesellschaft für Kommunikation mbH, Hamburg

avedition GmbH
Verlag für Architektur und Design
Senefelderstr. 109
70176 Stuttgart
Germany
Tel.: +49 (0)711 / 220 22 79-0
Fax: +49 (0)711 / 220 22 79-15
eventdesign@avedition.de
www.avedition.com

© Copyright 2018 av edition GmbH, Stuttgart

© Copyright of photos with individual companies, agencies and photographers

This work is subject to copyright. All rights are reserved, whether the whole or part of the material is concerned, and specifically but not exclusively the right of translation, reprinting, reuse of illustrations, recitation, broadcasting, reproduction on microfilms or in other ways, and storage in databases or any other media. For use of any kind, the written permission of the copyright owner must be obtained.

ISBN 978-3-89986-280-5

Redaktioneller Hinweis:
In einigen Fällen haben wir auf geschlechtsspezifische Begriffe verzichtet, um das Lesen zu vereinfachen. Falls wir die männliche Form von personenbezogenen Hauptwörtern gewählt haben, ist damit keine Herabwürdigung und /oder Diskriminierung weiblicher Personen beabsichtigt.